Life Is a Joke.

Life Is a Joke.

....

100 LIFE LESSONS
(with punch lines)

THE JAVNA BROTHERS

WORKMAN PUBLISHING · NEW YORK

Library of Congress Cataloging-in-Publication Data is available.

ISBN 978-1-5235-0007-9

Cover design: Vaughn Andrews
Cover spot photo by Andrzej Tokarski/Fotolia
Interior design: Janet Vicario

Workman books are available at special discounts when purchased in
bulk for premiums and sales promotions as well as for fund-raising or
educational use. Special editions or book excerpts also can be created to
specification. For details, contact the Special Sales Director at the address
below, or send an email to specialmarkets@workman.com.

Workman Publishing Co., Inc.
225 Varick Street
New York, NY 10014-4381
workman.com

WORKMAN is a registered trademark of Workman Publishing Co., Inc.

Printed in the United States of America
First printing September 2017

10 9 8 7 6 5 4 3 2 1

Contents

Introduction

What's the difference between a good joke and a great joke? The great ones not only make you laugh—they make you think.

For years, we've been using jokes to pass on practical life lessons to our kids and friends. And it really works. When people are laughing, they're open to ideas they'd probably just ignore from someone who was handing out "serious" advice.

At some point, it occurred to us that this could be the basis for a book—maybe even a whole new genre—a combination joke and self-help book.

That's how *Life Is a Joke* was born.

This collection includes a lot of our favorite jokes, plus a bunch suggested by family, friends . . . and even psychologists. You may have heard some of them before—they're classics— but we're betting you never looked at them quite this way. We think you'll be surprised at how relevant they can be to everyday life. We were. We often find ourselves referencing various punch lines to describe personal experiences—using them the way we recite favorite lines from songs or movies.

It turns out that these jokes and lessons are really just part of a universal human tradition. All cultures use little stories to teach and pass on wisdom. Aesop, for example, wrote his fables in ancient Greece 2,500 years ago. And Zen Buddhists began using parables called *koans* about 1,000 years ago to help reveal truths about the world. So now we think of great jokes as western koans. Or maybe Zen Cohens.

A FEW PRACTICAL TIPS ABOUT THE BOOK

1. **Although the jokes are numbered, there's really no order or hierarchy to them.** (It wasn't our idea. We suspect the publisher insisted on numbering them just to prove there really are 100.)

2. **If you're the kind of person who feels compelled to start on page one, go right ahead.** But for the rest of you, here's good news: We designed the book so you can start anywhere. Each joke/life lesson stands alone.

3. **We encourage you to read one joke at a time and savor the experience.** For one thing, it's a good way to get your money's worth—it'll make the book last longer. For another, you'll get a chance to really let each joke percolate in your brain and see how its message applies to you.

4. **Remember not to take this book (or *anything*, for that matter) too seriously.** After all, life is a joke.

The Javna Brothers
Ashland, Oregon

Life Is a Joke.

Force of Habit

*"The chains of habit are generally too small to be
felt until they are too strong to be broken."*
—Samuel Johnson

Two old pirates were sitting at a bar, talking about their adventures. "So," said one pirate, "how'd ye get that metal hook for a hand?"

"We were ransacking a merchant ship in the West Indies when I got into a sword fight with the ship's captain and he cut off my hand."

"Fantastic!" said the first pirate. "And how'd ye get that peg leg?"

"We were ransacking a schooner off Haiti when I got into hand-to-hand combat with the schooner's captain. He swung his sword with such force that he cut off my leg."

"Amazing!" said the first pirate. "And how'd ye get that patch over your right eye?"

"I was standing on the deck of my ship when a seagull crapped on my face."

"That's how you lost your eye?" asked the first pirate.

"Well, it was my first day with the hook."

LIFE LESSON

Nobody adjusts to big changes instantly. It takes time to get used to new conditions, and you're bound to make mistakes. But you don't have to be the guy with the hook. If you recognize changes as they're happening, you can limit your mistakes by developing new habits to go along with the new conditions. And surprisingly, you'll find that it doesn't take a lot of will-power to change a habit—just persistence.

BEYOND THE PUNCH LINE

It's a widely held myth that it takes twenty-one days to form a new habit. A 2009 study showed that new habits are actually more likely to take two to eight months. It also showed that success in creating a new habit depends largely on the consistency of repetitions at the beginning, not on how hard you work. You just have to keep at it. And if you forget every now and then? That doesn't seem to impact your progress at all. Creating a new habit can be fairly painless and stress-free, if you're willing to do the basic work. According to Charles Duhigg in *The Power of Habit*, it's a three-step process: 1. Create a trigger; 2. Pick a routine; 3. Enjoy the reward.

Step 1: The trigger is a reminder that tells you to start the process. It works best if you pick a regular part of your schedule and add to it. For example, say you're trying to take vitamins regularly. The trigger could be brushing your teeth. You tell yourself that every morning before you brush your teeth, you'll take vitamins. Or if you're trying to read more, you might tell yourself that when you sit down to lunch each day, you'll read for five minutes. The beauty of this is that it switches the burden from willpower to a reminder system.

Step 2: The routine is the action that constitutes the new habit—taking vitamins or reading, in the previous examples. Expert advice: Keep the routine as simple as possible to begin with. Take just one vitamin or read just one page. The easier it is to start, the better. Get the repetitions going, and worry about the quality of the effort later. The first and most important thing is to establish it as a routine in your life.

Step 3: The reward is whatever benefit or result you're aiming for. At first, it may just be the satisfaction of doing what you set out to do. Later, you'll get the benefit of the action itself— feeling better from the vitamins, the pleasure of reading a good novel, losing weight, etc.

Science has proven that these steps really work. All it takes is the effort.

Leave Me a Loan

*"I have not failed. I've just found
10,000 ways that won't work."*
—Thomas Edison

A wealthy woman goes into a New York City bank to ask for a loan. She tells the loan officer that she's going on vacation and needs to borrow $5,000. "Well," says the banker, "do you have anything you can use as collateral?"

"Yes, I do," the woman replies. "I'll use my Rolls-Royce."

"You mean you want to put up a $250,000 Rolls-Royce as collateral for a $5,000 loan?" asks the stunned banker.

The woman nods and hands over the keys. The loan officer can't believe she's for real, so he has an associate check her credentials to make sure she's the legitimate owner. Sure enough, everything checks out, so the banker parks the luxury car in the bank's underground garage and writes her a check for $5,000.

Two weeks later the woman comes back from vacation and immediately goes to the bank, where she pays off the $5,000 loan—along with $15.41 in interest. The loan officer takes the money, and as he's handing her the keys, he says, "Miss, we're glad to have your business, but we're puzzled. We did some research and found out you're a multimillionaire. So why would you need to borrow $5,000?"

The woman smiles and replies, "Where else in New York City could I park my car for two weeks for only $15.41 and expect it to be there when I return?"

LIFE LESSON

"Anyone can do it the conventional way" was one of our father's favorite lessons. He insisted that there are solutions to any problem—often simple ones, at that—which no one has tried yet. So if you approach problem solving with an open mind, and without preconceived ideas about what the solution *ought* to be, you can come up with some pretty impressive results.

BEYOND THE PUNCH LINE

Here are a few tricks to help you look "outside the box" for solutions:

• **Make it someone else's problem.** Studies indicate that we tend to be more creative when we're solving other people's problems than when we're trying to solve our own. So imagine yourself giving advice to a friend with the same problem.

• **Turn the problem upside down.** Look at it from a completely different point of view. Try literally turning your paper upside down or studying an object or a plan from a different angle. Imagine that a minor result is actually your goal. This kind of thinking can help you to see details or patterns you might otherwise miss, which may help you find a solution.

• **Study the problem, not the solution.** Take the time to really understand the problem, and the solutions may become clearer. Albert Einstein said: "If I had an hour to solve a problem and my life depended on the answer, I would spend the first fifty-five minutes figuring out the proper questions to ask. For if I knew the proper questions, I could solve the problem in less than five minutes."

• **Reverse the process.** Start with the solution you're hoping for and work backward to where you are now, step by step. According to one expert, "This forces the brain to think in a different way.... The brain is almost always more active when it comes to novel stimuli and information."

• **And if all else fails, ask a kid.** If the problem is something a child can understand, ask them how *they* would solve the problem. Even if you don't get a viable answer, a child's unconventional thinking may prod you into seeing a solution that you wouldn't have thought of yourself.

Great Expectations

*"The first and most difficult risk we can take
is to be honest with ourselves."*
—Walter Anderson

An eighty-year-old man was at the doctor's office for his annual checkup. The doctor asked him how he was feeling. "Never better," the man replied. "I've got a twenty-year-old bride and she's pregnant with my child. What do you think of that, Doc?"

The doctor thought for a minute and said, "Let me tell you a story. My brother-in-law is an avid hunter. One day, he was in such a hurry to go hunting that he accidentally grabbed an umbrella instead of his rifle. So there he was, walking in the woods, when a grizzly bear suddenly appeared in front of him. He quickly raised the umbrella, pointed it at the bear, and squeezed the handle."

"What happened then?" the old man asked.

"Well," said the doctor, "believe it or not, the bear fell dead on the ground."

"Impossible!" exclaimed the old man. "Someone else must've shot the bear."

"Exactly my point," replied the doctor.

LIFE LESSON

There's a big difference between having self-confidence and lying to yourself. It may be tough to recognize which is which, but it's essential to develop that critical judgment. Experiencing real happiness often depends on having reasonable expectations (see Joke 98).

BEYOND THE PUNCH LINE

To keep your expectations reasonable:

1. **Start by asking what they are.** Sometimes we have a vague idea of what we expect, but haven't really defined it yet. If you can clearly articulate your expectations, it will be much easier to evaluate them.

2. **Ask yourself where they came from.** Are they based on experience and observation . . . or did you just make them up? Be honest about it. If there's a gap between what you *know* happens in the real world and what you *hope* will happen, it's probably time to adjust your expectations.

3. **Share them.** If your expectations involve other people, do they know about it? We often develop expectations of other people and then "forget" to tell them—a recipe for failure. Check in with potential partners before things go south; share thoughts and see if they want to participate.

4. **Get feedback.** Use friends as sounding boards to help gauge whether your expectations are reasonable. Ask them what they think. If they burst out laughing when they hear what you expect from life, it's probably a good sign you need to do some reevaluating.

Don't Confuse Me with Facts

*"A lot of good arguments are spoiled by some fool
who knows what he is talking about."*
—Miguel de Unamuno

A man is convinced he's dead. His wife tells him he's not dead. His kids tell him he's not dead. His friends tell him he's not dead. But he still insists he is. Finally, at their wits' end, the family talks him into seeing a psychiatrist.

The psychiatrist decides that his best strategy for curing the man is to convince him to accept one fact: Dead men do not bleed. Over the next six months, he has the man study medical textbooks and anatomy charts, all of which support the psychiatrist's point. Then, he has the man observe autopsies, dissect cadavers, and work as an assistant in a funeral home. Finally the exasperated man says to the psychiatrist, "Okay. Enough already. I get it: Dead men do not bleed."

The psychiatrist smiles, and then takes the man's hand and pricks the end of his finger with a needle. As a drop of blood oozes out, the man looks at his finger and says, "Well, what do you know! Dead men *do* bleed!"

LIFE LESSON

Logic doesn't always win out. Studies have proven that we'll often ignore facts—or twist them—if they don't support our views. So if you're trying to win an argument and expect to get the other person to change their mind, you're probably wasting your time. You may be right, but being right has nothing to do with it—people believe what they want to believe.

BEYOND THE PUNCH LINE

It might seem crazy that a person would cling to a belief in the face of incontrovertible evidence, but it's so common that scientists have coined a term for it: "the backfire effect." The reason: Attempting to correct people's misconceptions will often *backfire* and bind them even more strongly to their erroneous beliefs.

• **This has been demonstrated many times.** In a 2006 study, for example, subjects were given two newspaper articles: The first one supported their beliefs with incorrect data; the second one corrected the misinformation. Rather than changing their views in any way, subjects decided the *second* article was incorrect . . . and even tended to see a conspiracy behind the correction.

• **It's not merely anecdotal:** Brain scans have confirmed these results. When subjects in an MRI test were shown information that confirmed what they already thought about a particular topic, areas of the brain associated with learning lit up. But when the same subjects were shown info that contradicted their beliefs, sections of the brain that are associated with "thought suppression" lit up. This illustrates how difficult it is to change anyone's mind once it's made up. It's not just about logic; it's biology.

• So is it possible to change people's minds at all? Maybe. Researchers say:

1. People will listen to (though not necessarily accept) new information if an issue affects their lives directly. If they've got no skin in the game, they'll tune it out and stick with prior beliefs.

2. People are more likely to weigh new evidence seriously (and even change their views) when they're deliberating with a small group. In one study, people working in small groups changed their minds 75 percent more frequently than when deliberating alone.

3. People who are asked to explain how their ideas work in the real world may realize how little they know about a subject and modify their beliefs. On the other hand, people who are asked to explain *why* they believe something are likely to become more adamant about their beliefs.

5

The Big Picture

"To change ourselves effectively,
we first had to change our perceptions."
—Steven Covey

A few minutes into a morning flight from Boston to Chicago, the passengers were startled by a sudden jolt. The captain came on the intercom and announced, "No need for alarm, folks. We lost an engine, but that just means we'll be an hour late getting to Chicago."

The passengers grumbled, but then settled in for the longer flight . . . except for the guy in seat 12D. "Oh, great," he said loudly. "I'd better not miss my 3:00 p.m. meeting!"

A short while later there was another jolt. "Nothing to worry about," said the captain. "We lost another engine, but that just means we'll be *two* hours late."

Again, the passengers took the news quietly . . . except for the guy in 12D. "Outrageous!" he exclaimed. "As soon as we land, I'm calling customer service!"

A few minutes later there was another jolt, and the captain announced, "Uh . . . sorry to tell you, folks, our third engine just quit. But don't worry—we've still got one good one, and we'll still make it to Chicago. The only thing is, we're going to be *three* hours late."

Still everyone remained calm . . . except for 12D. "If I miss this meeting," he said loudly enough for everyone on the entire plane to hear, "this airline will be hearing from my lawyer!"

Ten minutes later there was an even bigger jolt. "Oh my God!" shouted the captain, "we just lost engine number four!"

"Well, this is just great!" the guy in 12D grumbled. "Now we'll be up here all day!"

LIFE LESSON

Of course, this is the worst possible scenario; the guy is doomed. But he doesn't *realize* he's doomed because he's measuring events with the wrong metric—his schedule instead of his life. That kind of myopia is pervasive in all of our lives. It's easy to get sucked in by the small stuff and miss the bigger picture. Things may actually be rosier than you think—or they may be darker. But you'll never know unless you take a step back every once in a while and see what's going on.

BEYOND THE PUNCH LINE

Learning to see the big picture is no different than developing any new skill. You're developing a new way of thinking, and that takes practice and patience. If you're going to give it a shot, you'll need a place to start. See if one of these ideas works for you:

1. **Seek out a friend or mentor whose life history is completely different from yours.** Tell them about the challenges you're facing. Ask if they've had similar problems, and if so, how they've dealt with them. That might help you see things from a different perspective.

2. **Set aside an hour or two every week to disengage from daily concerns.** Take a walk or hang out in a coffee shop; use the time to ponder the week ahead and make plans. If you find you're off course, this is a good time to make changes.

3. **Every few days take some time—ten or fifteen minutes is plenty—to write down your thoughts.** Don't make it a to-do list. You're reflecting on what's important to you, not on what you have to get done.

4. **If you're the kind of person who tends to get discouraged by the things you haven't done, make a conscious effort to notice the things you *have* done.** Doing that will give you a bigger—and truer—picture of your life.

Feet of Clay

*"If I had to choose a superhero to be,
I would pick Superman. He's everything that I'm not."*
—**Stephen Hawking**

Two half-drunk guys are in a bar at the top of a skyscraper. The first guy says, "You know, I believe that if I had just one more beer, I could fly."

The other guy says, "That's impossible!"

"No, really," says the first guy. He orders another beer and drinks it down, walks over to the balcony—and jumps off. He starts falling, falling, falling . . . but just before he hits the ground, he stops in midair and flies gracefully back to the top of the building.

"Wow!" says the second guy. "You know, if I had another beer, I bet I could do that too." He downs his beer, runs over to the balcony, takes a flying leap . . . and hits the sidewalk with a *splat*.

The bartender turns to the first guy and says, "You know, Superman, you can be a real jerk when you drink."

LIFE LESSON
We all have heroes—people who represent our highest personal ambitions and values. We tend to idealize them, but

remember—they're just people. They can be jerks, just like anyone. They make mistakes, just like anyone. And if you expect too much of them, they'll let you down—just like anyone.

Love your heroes for the things they've accomplished. But don't ascribe traits to them that they don't have. Hero worship isn't healthy for you ... or for them.

BEYOND THE PUNCH LINE

Three ways to keep heroes in perspective:

1. **Think about who your heroes are, and why.** Remind yourself what it is about your hero that attracted you in the first place. What does he or she embody that's meaningful to you? How do your heroes inspire you and how can you make these ideals part of your life?

2. **Be realistic about them.** A hero's personal weaknesses could make them even more admirable, because they've managed to accomplish remarkable things—despite their flaws. On the other hand, they may have done things too repugnant to tolerate. If that's the case, admit it to yourself and move on.

3. **Focus on yourself.** Understand the difference between heroes and role models. We don't expect to become heroes, but we do aspire to be like our role models. We admire heroes for their extraordinary achievements; we admire role models because they deal with the challenges of everyday life in ways that make them better people. Heroes perform on a global stage. Role models live in our neighborhood. They're teachers, mentors, parents—people who care about us and are part of our lives. So ... perhaps more of our role models should be our heroes as well.

7

Good Enough?

"The privilege of a lifetime is being who you are."
—Joseph Campbell

A woman in her late forties suffers a massive heart attack and is rushed to the hospital for emergency surgery. On the operating table she has a near-death experience—and sees God. "Is this the end for me?" she asks.

"No, child," replies God. "You have another thirty-seven years to live."

The woman recovers from the surgery, and knowing she has so much more time on Earth, she decides to make the most of it. So she stays in the hospital to get a facelift, liposuction, and a tummy tuck. When her last operation is done, the doctors discharge her from the hospital. As she's leaving, she crosses the street, is hit by a truck, and dies. Arriving in heaven, she sees God and complains, "You said I had another thirty-seven years. Why didn't you save me from that truck?"

"Oh, sorry," God says. "I didn't recognize you."

LIFE LESSON

There will always be things we can criticize about ourselves—our looks, intelligence, weight, bad habits, lack of success. But at some point, we need to be able to say, "This is who I am" and celebrate the life we've been given. You may not have everything you want, but if you've got something good, don't take it for granted; treat it with respect.

BEYOND THE PUNCH LINE

Are you overly self-critical? Here are some quick tips for learning to appreciate the person you are:

• **Don't try to "fix" yourself.** If you're trying to fix yourself, it means you think you're broken. That's the opposite of self-acceptance.

• **Be realistic.** Some things about your life can be changed, but some—such as your family and certain health problems—can't. If you're trying to change the unchangeable, you're setting yourself up to fail. And when you fail, you'll blame yourself for being not good enough.

• **Volunteer to help others.** One thing we all understand and appreciate is the power of a helping hand. No matter how you see yourself, knowing that you can help someone else will add to your sense of self-worth.

• **Respect your life.** Check out what you do every day, what it takes to survive, and how much you put into it. You may want something more for yourself in the long run, but self-respect begins with appreciating how much you already do right.

8

Sorry, Frog

"Rejection doesn't have to mean you aren't good enough;
it often just means the other person
failed to notice what you have to offer."
—Ash Sweeney

An engineer is crossing the road when he hears a frog calling out to him, "Hey, mister. If you kiss me, I'll turn into a beautiful princess." The engineer bends down, picks up the frog, and puts it in his pocket. The frog speaks up again. "Hey, didn't you hear me? I tell you what—if you kiss me and turn me back into a beautiful princess, I'll be your girlfriend for a week." The engineer takes the frog out of his pocket, smiles at it, and puts it back in his pocket. So the frog cries out, "Okay, okay. If you kiss me and turn me back into a princess, I'll do anything you say." Again the engineer takes the frog out, smiles at it, and puts it back into his pocket. Finally, the frog asks, "What's the matter with you? I've told you I'm a beautiful princess. I'll be your girlfriend. I'll do whatever you say. What more do you want?"

The engineer smiles and says, "Look, I'm an engineer. I don't have time for a girlfriend. But a talking frog—now, that's cool."

LIFE LESSON

It's sad, but true: No matter how irresistible what you're offering (including yourself) may seem to *you*, not everyone is going to want it. Don't take it personally and don't let the experience change how you think of yourself; people have their own reasons for making choices. All you can do is try to get them to see things your way. And if that doesn't work, keep looking. It will be that much more rewarding when you find someone you connect with.

BEYOND THE PUNCH LINE

It's not a personal failing that makes rejection feel so painful—it's your body. A 2015 University of Michigan study discovered that we process social rejection in the same area of the brain that registers physical pain. "These results give new meaning to the idea that social rejection 'hurts,'" the researchers explained. "On the surface, spilling a hot cup of coffee on yourself and thinking about how rejected you feel . . . may seem to elicit very different types of pain. But this research shows that they [are] similar."

The paradox is that although we can't help taking rejection personally, it's seldom intended that way. One writer shares the story of holding an audition for a part in a television show. After the casting directors picked the actor, he overheard two rejected applicants wondering what they did wrong. The answer: nothing. The directors were getting hungry and just picked the next qualified actor who showed up so they could go to lunch.

Of course, knowing it wasn't intended doesn't minimize the pain. But it can help you understand that rejection doesn't mean there's something wrong with you or your work—everyone is rejected at some point. Treat rejection like a wound that needs to heal. Give it time and medicine—whatever's appropriate for you. And then get up and try again.

—— 9 ——

Efficiency Expert

"There is nothing so useless as doing efficiently that which should not be done at all."
—Peter F. Drucker

An efficiency expert concluded his lecture to a group of business leaders with a note of caution: "You need to be careful about trying these techniques at home."

"Why?" asked a man in the audience.

"Well," the expert explained, "I watched my wife's routine at dinner for years. She made lots of trips between the refrigerator, stove, table, and cabinets, often carrying a single item at a time. One day I told her, 'You're wasting too much time. Why don't you try carrying several things at once?' "

"Did it save time?" the guy in the audience asked.

"Actually, yes," replied the expert. "It used to take her twenty minutes to make dinner. Now I do it in ten."

LIFE LESSON

Rather than expressing appreciation to his wife for having made (and served) dinner, the guy in the joke critiqued her efficiency. You can imagine how that made her feel—which brings us to this basic lesson: Don't forget to say thank you.

Studies show that thanking someone is a powerful way to connect with them. It's fast, it's easy, and it gets results. (You'd think an efficiency expert would know that.) But more important, it makes life more satisfying. As the French philosopher Alfred Painter wrote, "Saying thank you is more than good manners. It is good spirituality."

BEYOND THE PUNCH LINE

• In 2010, professors from Harvard and the University of Pennsylvania conducted a major study on the benefits of thanking someone, in which subjects were asked to help a student. The study found that when the subjects were thanked, they were more responsive to additional requests from the student and twice as likely to offer assistance to other people. The testers' conclusion: "People weren't providing more help because they felt better or because it boosted their self-esteem, but because they appreciated being needed and felt more socially valued when they'd been thanked." Being thanked made them feel more fulfilled and made them better citizens.

• But that's not all. A 2014 study found that saying thank you also plays a key role in social interaction. This study, explains one of the lead researchers, "was the first to show evidence that . . . an expression of gratitude can help to initiate a new relationship. A simple thank-you leads people to view you as a warmer human being and, consequently, to be more interested in socially engaging with you and continuing to get to know you."

• This may be why "thanks" is the most-used one-word sentence in the English language . . . and why "thank you" is the most-used two-word sentence.

10

Brain Freeze

"If you panic, that's a good way to lose.
You have to stay in control."
—**Ted Turner**

After his theory of relativity made him world famous, Albert Einstein was in demand as a speaker at universities around the country. Einstein didn't drive, so he depended on his chauffeur to take him to his speaking engagements. After one lecture, the chauffeur—who bore a striking physical resemblance to Einstein—commented, "I've heard your lecture so many times, Professor Einstein, that I could probably deliver it for you!"

"Really?" laughed Einstein. "Well, we're going to Yale next week. Let's do it there."

Sure enough, the chauffeur delivered a perfect rendition of Einstein's standard lecture, while Einstein gleefully sat in the back of the room wearing his chauffeur's uniform. But just as the driver was leaving the podium, a particularly snotty graduate student stood up and asked a complicated question about antimatter formation, hoping to trip up the great scientist. Without missing a beat, the chauffeur replied, "Sir, the answer to that question is simple—so simple, in fact, that I will let my chauffeur answer it for me."

LIFE LESSON

When it seems like you're backed into a corner, don't give up. Even in the worst situations, there's always a chance you can find a way out . . . if you stay calm. The trick is to ignore the noise of panic so that you can hear the practical voice in your head and come up with a solution. This doesn't come easily for many of us, but anyone can learn to do it. And if you find yourself in an unexpectedly tough situation, you'll be glad you did.

BEYOND THE PUNCH LINE

One of the reasons it's tough to think straight under pressure is that when we're stressed, our brains release a chemical called cortisol, which causes cloudy thinking. Ironically, we don't *realize* we're not thinking straight . . . because our brains are cloudy.

One way to minimize this effect is to practice clear thinking under stress. Neuroscientist Daniel Levitan suggests doing a "pre-mortem"—that is, trying to figure out in advance what can go wrong with any situation so that you can prepare for it. This is a way to feel more in control, which helps you keep your cool in a tight situation. As one researcher puts it: "Anything that increases your *perception of control* over a situation— whether it actually increases your control or not—can substantially decrease your stress level." A pre-mortem might include:

• **Imagining the toughest questions** people will ask in a business or social situation and rehearsing answers to them.

• **Developing a clear sense** of your boundaries, and how to assert them. For instance, if you're uncomfortable talking about religion, be prepared to gracefully change the subject if someone brings it up.

• **Trying to envision** any unintended consequences that might occur in a situation and how they can be managed.

And if nothing else works, try using a good-luck charm. Believe it or not, research indicates that a person with a lucky charm will generally perform better on a test than a person who doesn't have one. Why? Because a good-luck piece gives them a sense of control.

11

The Old Sandbag Trick

"What I say is misdirection. What you see is an illusion."
—Amit Kalantri

A man rides up to the Mexico-US border on his bicycle, carrying two large bags on his shoulders. The American border guard asks, "What's in the bags?"

"Sand," the man answers.

"I'll bet," the guard sneers. "Let me see." So he takes the bags, empties them, and finds . . . just sand. Unconvinced, he has the sand analyzed, and finds it contains . . . nothing. It's just sand. The man with the bicycle gathers up the sand, puts it back in the bags, and crosses the border.

A week later, the same thing happens. "What's in the bags?" the border guard demands. "Sand," the man replies.

The guard still doesn't believe him, so he does another analysis. Sure enough, the bags contain only sand. The man with the bicycle repacks his bags and rides across the border.

This weekly routine continues for about a year. Then it stops. A few months later, the border guard walks into a local café and spots the "sand man" having lunch. He goes up to the man and says, "Hey, I know you were smuggling *something*. The curiosity is killing me. Please tell me—what was it."

The man takes a sip of coffee, smiles at the border guard, and says, "Bicycles."

LIFE LESSON

We're all suckers for what magicians call *misdirection*— "a form of deception in which an audience's attention is focused on one thing in order to distract it from another." It's surprising how often this comes up in life—particularly in business and politics. When misdirection is done well, you might not notice it's happening at all. But when you do notice it—when something is bothering you and your BS radar goes off—don't ignore that feeling. Deconstruct the situation and find out what you're missing. It's an effective way to keep from becoming a victim.

BEYOND THE PUNCH LINE

Misdirection works because of an innate human quality called *inattentional blindness*. Research has shown that if we're not paying attention to something, our brains won't register having seen it at all . . . even if it's right in front of our eyes. So if someone is using misdirection to get your attention *away* from something, they'll probably do it by subtly getting you to look *toward* something else. In everyday conversation, for example, it might show up as someone responding to a direct question by changing the topic . . . or by getting angry instead of answering it—and even making you feel defensive for having asked it in the first place. Being alert to this kind of "bait and switch" in your interactions with others is your best defense against it. Keep your eyes and ears peeled. Misdirection is everywhere.

—— **12** ——

Piece of Cake

"Tell me what you brag about and I'll tell you what you lack."
—**Spanish proverb**

Three families—the Gencarellis, the DiRienzos, and the Volpes—have all had bakeries on the same block in Florence, Italy, for generations. But after years of peaceful coexistence, the Gencarelli family declares "war" and puts a sign in their shop window saying: "We make the best cakes in Italy." The DiRienzo family fights back and puts a sign in *their* window proclaiming: "We make the best cakes in the world." Finally, the Volpe family quietly posts this sign outside their shop: "We make the best cakes on the block."

LIFE LESSON
Being competitive is human nature. We're always trying to make ourselves appear taller, smarter, stronger, and just plain better than the competition. But this can also backfire. People recognize insincere self-promotion for what it is and

appreciate modesty. A willingness to acknowledge personal limitations and "think small" shows real confidence . . . and it wins people over.

BEYOND THE PUNCH LINE

Are you a braggart? Sure, bragging and self-promotion are annoying . . . when others do it. But according to a 2015 British study, you may not be aware that other people have that same response when *you* do it. "When we engage in self-promotion, we tend to overestimate other people's positive reactions and underestimate their negative ones," says the study's lead author. "It may be beneficial . . . to try to realize that people may actually be less happy than [you] think to hear about [your] latest achievement."

In other words, one reason we brag is that we don't know any better. We think we're sharing information that people will welcome. Instead, we trigger the opposite reaction and drive people away. It's a blind spot we all have (see Joke 41).

The study also suggests that the harder we try to be convincing, the more inflated our claims become—and as a result, people are even less inclined to trust us. As University of Massachusetts professor Dr. Susan Whitbourne explains: "How do I know you're telling the truth when you claim to have achieved some great outcome? If you don't give me hard evidence, I have to rely on your word alone. People don't trust claims they can't verify."

13

Fast Friends

"If you lend a friend five dollars and
never see him again, it was worth it."
—**Anonymous**

T wo campers are walking through the woods when they suddenly see a huge brown bear in the clearing ahead. The bear sees the campers too and begins to head toward them. The first guy quickly digs a pair of sneakers out of his backpack and frantically begins to put them on.

"What are you doing?" asks the second guy. "Sneakers won't help you outrun a bear."

"I don't need to outrun the bear," the first guy replies. "I just need to outrun you."

LIFE LESSON

No matter how close you are to someone, there are going to be times when your interests and theirs diverge. That's when it's important to have a clear idea of what the relationship means to you—because at that point, you're going to have to choose a path: Should you stick together as a team and sacrifice your own interests to help your friend? Or give up on the relationship and just try to outrun them?

PS: Remember that you're not the only one who has a choice. Your "friend" has the same decisions to make.

BEYOND THE PUNCH LINE

If you're trying to decide whether a friendship is worth saving, asking yourself these questions might help you figure it out:

1. **Is your friend interested in what you have to say** . . . or does every conversation somehow wind up being about them?

2. **Are you friends because you choose to be** . . . or because of circumstance? A lot of "friendships" are just a matter of convenience or proximity—for example, a carpooling buddy, or a partner in a school activity.

3. **Do you look forward to being together** . . . or do you dread it? Some people's lives are ongoing soap operas that make friendship feel more like a burden than a gift.

4. **Are they supportive** . . . or competitive? You can learn a lot by observing how friends respond to your good fortune and success.

5. **Do they praise you** . . . or put you down? Friends should be advocates for each other—in private *and* in front of other people.

6. **Do you feel close** . . . or is there an "invisible barrier" you can't break through? Some friendships seem to have limits that keep you feeling distant, even if you're trying to get closer. At some point you need to either accept it, try to change it, or put on your running shoes.

14

In Too Deep

"The human brain is a complex organ with the wonderful power of enabling man to find reasons for continuing to believe whatever it is that he wants to believe."
—Voltaire

An out-of-work actor goes into a doctor's office. "What seems to be wrong?" asks the doctor.

The man rolls up his sleeve and shows him a horrible rash covering his entire arm, from his armpit to his fingertips. "Wow!" says the MD. "How'd you get that?"

"Well, Doc, I got a job at the circus. I clean out the elephant cages, so I'm usually up to my ankles in poop. And if that isn't bad enough, sometimes the elephants get constipated and I have to give them suppositories, which means I have to stick my arm up the elephants' butts," replied the man. "That's how I got the rash."

"That's a *terrible* job!" says the doctor. "For God's sake, why don't you find some other line of work?"

"What? And give up show business?"

LIFE LESSON

To some extent, we all live in denial, deluding ourselves about who we are and what we're really doing. Studies have shown, for example, that although 66 percent of Americans are overweight, more than half of those people think they aren't; 93 percent of American drivers are sure they're above average; and even 94 percent of our teachers—who deal in facts—believe they're "in the top 50 percent of their profession." So the question isn't whether you're deluding yourself—it's how much and how it's affecting your life. If, like the guy in the joke, you're a slave to your delusion and erroneously believe you're already where you want to be, it could be stopping your personal growth. So challenge your perception. Try to see your life as it really is—and then learn to accept it . . . or change it.

BEYOND THE PUNCH LINE

According to a CBS News report, "On a scale of one to ten, you probably think you're a seven. And you wouldn't be alone." The point (and the title of the report): "Everyone Thinks They're Above Average." Studies of the phenomenon, known as *illusory superiority*, have led psychologists to three conclusions about why so many of us delude ourselves:

1. **People don't tell us** what they *really* think of our performance, so we assume we're better than we really are.

2. **Incompetent people** (and we're all incompetent at something) can't tell a good performance from a poor one, so they assume they're doing great.

3. **It preserves our sanity.** If we knew how lousy we really are at some things, our self-esteem would take a massive hit . . . which could undermine everything else we try to do.

So what's the harm in self-delusion? Consider a news report from New Zealand about a man who received thirty-two traffic tickets over five years—all for not wearing a seat belt. Rather than simply buckling up, he decided to circumvent the law by creating a fake seat belt that draped over his shoulder and made it *look* like he was wearing one. He thought he was fooling the authorities, but he actually was fooling himself. When he was killed in a head-on car crash in 2008, the police determined that the man's death could have been avoided . . . if he'd been wearing a seat belt.

— 15 —

Some Pig

"You may not control all the events that happen to you, but you can decide not to be reduced by them."
—Maya Angelou

A man was walking down a country road when he came to a farmhouse. Out front was a farmer, and standing beside him was a pig with a wooden leg.

"Hello," said the man. "Nice-looking pig you got there."

"Nice?" said the farmer. "He's the best darn pig in the world! Why, one time a huge bale of hay fell on me, and just when I thought I would suffocate to death, this pig rushed over, grabbed me by my foot, and pulled me out. Saved my life."

"Wow," said the man. "That's impressive."

"And another time," continued the farmer, "when the house caught fire, the pig rushed in and pulled both of my two kids to safety."

"That's amazing," said the man. "But I have to ask: What's with the wooden leg?"

"Well," the farmer answered, "when you've got a pig that special, you don't eat it all at once!"

LIFE LESSON

We like to think that when we help someone, they're going to show their appreciation in some way. Plenty of people will say thank you and mean it . . . but not everyone. Some people are simply unable to acknowledge that something's been done for them or express gratitude in a meaningful way. And though they may appreciate your efforts on some level, they still see you as a resource to exploit rather than as a human being. Like the farmer in the joke, they will use you up, piece by piece, unless you have the good sense to get away from them.

BEYOND THE PUNCH LINE

Here are a few signs that you're being taken advantage of by a supervisor or a friend:

1. They keep asking you to do more—help with another chore or loan them something else, or at work, put in more hours or take on extra tasks. They see you as someone they can exploit, so they use you for as many things as they can.

2. They make promises and then don't follow through. It's easy for a friend or coworker to tell you what you want to hear, but if there's consistently no action after they say yes, they're just stringing you along.

3. They never return a favor. Saying thank you is a good start, but if you help them and they never reciprocate, they're using you.

4. Someone else gets the credit. Did your supervisor claim credit for a job you did? Did your friend cite all the members of his committee and "forget" to mention you? If you think it's an oversight, let them know. If it's not an oversight, be prepared: They're probably going to do it again.

Still not sure? Trust your instincts. If it feels like you're being taken advantage of, you probably are.

16

Go with the Flow

*"Sometimes time spent reinventing the wheel results in
a revolutionary new rolling device. But sometimes it
just amounts to time spent reinventing the wheel."*
—**Steve Krug**

An old guy is driving home from work when his wife calls him on his cell phone. "Phil," she shouts in a panic, "Please be careful! I just heard on the news that some lunatic is driving the wrong way on Route 80."

"Hell, Doris, it's not just one car," he replies. "It's hundreds of them!"

LIFE LESSON

We live in a society that preaches rugged individualism and rewards entrepreneurial thinking. So it's easy to fall into the trap of believing that going your own way is automatically better than following the crowd. It can be, but wise people know you don't need to reinvent everything—sometimes there's a good reason why everyone is doing it that way: Because it works. In business, that's called *best practices*.

Next time you're wondering how to proceed, look around. If you see that everyone is doing it differently than you, consider whether *you're* the one who's going the wrong way. If you are, don't be afraid to turn around and go with the flow. It's never too late to head in the right direction.

BEYOND THE PUNCH LINE

So when is it better to follow the conventional path and when is it better to go your own way? Here are three questions to ask yourself when you're trying to decide whether it's a good idea to go along with the crowd:

1. **Will it save you time? Coming up with your own solutions takes a lot of effort, making and correcting mistakes as you go.** It can be a valuable learning experience, but isn't always worth the time it takes. So which is more valuable to you: the time or the experience?

2. **Will it make you feel better? Reinventing the wheel is mentally draining work.** The struggle can make you miserable and grumpy. Taking the conventional route might be less stressful and can leave you feeling more ready to take on the next challenge.

3. **Will it save resources? Few of us have unlimited resources, so it's important to figure out how to use the ones we have most effectively.** The conventional route may save you money, energy, and labor, enabling you to use them more strategically in the future.

17

Countdown

"Any day above ground is a good day."
—Robert Gerus

A doctor walks into the examining room and puts his hand on his patient's shoulder.

"I'm afraid I have some bad news. You're dying, and you don't have much time left."

"Oh no!" replies the patient. "How long do I have to live?"

"Ten," says the doctor.

"Ten?" cries the panicked patient. "Ten what? Days? Weeks? Months?"

The doctor calmly replies, "Nine . . ."

LIFE LESSON
"Time is quickly slipping away" is a message we hear frequently but tend to forget. Use this joke to remind yourself of how fleeting life is and how important it is to appreciate the time we have.

BEYOND THE PUNCH LINE
We don't think the idea needs more commentary, but here's another way to say it: carpe diem. It's a Latin term that comes from the Roman poet Horace (65 BC-8 BC). The literal quote is *carpe diem quam minimum credula postero*—"pluck the day,

trusting as little as possible in the next one." But over time, it's become commonly known as "seize the day"—a concise exhortation to make the most of the time you have. And if that's too obscure for you, the Hebrew version of the phrase is even more direct. It translates as: "If not now, when?"

—— 18 ——

Buy, Buy, Baby

"Pretend that every single person you meet has a sign around his or her neck that says, 'Make me feel important.' Not only will you succeed in sales, you will succeed in life."
—Mary Kay Ash

Corporal Jesse had the gift of gab, so his captain assigned him to the military induction center, where his job was to advise new recruits about their government benefits, especially their GI insurance. Before long the captain noticed that Jesse was selling supplemental insurance to 99 percent of the recruits—an incredible sign-up rate. The captain wanted to know how Jesse was doing it, so he stood in the back of the room and listened to the corporal's sales pitch.

"Men," Jesse explained to the inductees, "if you have the standard GI insurance and get killed in battle, the government pays your beneficiaries a maximum of

$20,000. But if you have the *supplemental* insurance, the government has to pay $200,000."

"So let me ask you," he concluded, "which group do you think they're going to send into battle first?"

LIFE LESSON

Like a lot of people, you may be uncomfortable with the idea of "selling." But whether you realize it or not, you've been doing it all your life. In fact, any time you have to convince someone to go along with *anything*, you're using the same basic skills as the guy selling insurance. Trying to get a friend to volunteer at the food bank? Trying to get your kids to go do their homework? Trying to get your boss to give you next Friday off? The challenge is always the same: You have to show the listener what's in it for them and answer their implicit question, "Why do I care?" The more focused you are on answering that question, the more effective your "sales pitch" will be.

BEYOND THE PUNCH LINE

Here are four basic rules for developing a better sales pitch:

1. **Know your purpose.** What are you trying to achieve? Your whole pitch depends on being clear about this. If you're not sure, how can you communicate it?

2. **Know your audience.** Understand as much as you can (or as much as is warranted) about what your "customer" wants and what motivates them. Try to anticipate their objections.

Some experts say developing empathy is the key to understanding your audience, and the best way to do that is to ask questions. Ask about their situation, their concerns, their goals, and most important, how you can help. Then listen. "Keep listening," says one, "until you have a clear understanding of the whole picture."

3. **Know what you're "selling."** Whatever you're selling—a product, a program, or even an idea—know it inside out and backward before you open your mouth. And while you're at it, make sure you understand it from the "customer's" perspective.

Every transaction has a practical component and an emotional component. The emotional aspect is the prime decision maker. Corporal Jesse, for example, was selling insurance—but what appealed to his customers was that he was offering security and even a survival strategy.

4. **Make a connection.** People don't trust strangers—they trust someone they have a personal relationship with. So develop a relationship with your audience. Be nice, be helpful, be funny (tell them a joke), be patient, and above all, be genuine. If they relate to you, they'll trust you, and they'll practically do the selling *for* you.

Insufficient Information

"The explanation requiring the fewest assumptions is most likely to be correct."
—William of Ockham (Occam's razor)

A nurse who worked for a local home health agency was out making her daily rounds when her car suddenly ran out of gas. Luckily, she was only a block from a gas station, so she quickly walked over and asked the attendant to lend her a gas can. The attendant told her he was sorry—he had only one gas can and someone else had just borrowed it. In a hurry and desperate to get back on the road, the nurse went back to her car to look for some other container to hold the gas, but the only thing she could find in the car was a bedpan. So she took the bedpan to the station, had the attendant fill it with gas, and brought it back to her car. Just as she started pouring the gas from the bedpan into her car, two businessmen who happened to be driving by stopped, gawking in disbelief.

"Wow," said one, "that nurse is going to make a fortune!"

LIFE LESSON

It makes sense, doesn't it? You see someone pouring something from a bedpan and assume it's pee. We make perfectly "logical" assumptions like that all the time. The problem is that our conclusions are often wrong.

This behavior is so common that there's a psychological term for it: *jumping to conclusions bias*, or *JTC* for short (really). JTC is probably an inborn trait that has helped us survive since prehistoric times—so we're not likely to stop it anytime soon. But we can be aware that we do it and try to catch some of our crazier "conclusions" before they escape into the world. That's not just a way to avoid looking foolish—it's also a way to protect yourself from making damaging decisions based on "information" you simply made up.

BEYOND THE PUNCH LINE

Research shows that the best way to avoid JTC is to demand the same kind of proof from yourself that you'd ask for from others. That's not always easy, so try memorizing these four questions and then ask them when you need to take a closer look at a conclusion:

1. What are the facts? List them.

2. Are they really facts or are you letting your emotions color what you see?

3. Based on the "evidence," would other people come to the same conclusion?

4. Imagine a specific friend presenting you with the same conclusion. What would you say to them—is it the same thing you're saying to yourself?

— 20 —

Too Much Information

"The best time for you to hold your tongue is the time you feel you must say something or bust."
—Josh Billings

A sales rep, a clerk, and a manager are on their way to lunch when they find an antique oil lamp. They rub it—and to their astonishment, a genie emerges. "Whew! I'm so glad to be out of there," he says, "that I'll give each of you one wish." The clerk excitedly shouts, "Me first, me first! I want to be blissfully happy sitting at an outdoor café in Paris, drinking coffee with the love of my life." And *poof*! She's gone. The other two stare incredulously at the empty space. Then the sales rep shouts, "Me next, me next! I want to be in the Bahamas, sitting on a beach with a personal masseuse, drinking piña coladas without a care in the world." And *poof*! He's gone. Then the genie looks over to the manager and says, "Your turn." The manager smiles and says, "I want those two back in the office after lunch."

LIFE LESSON

It's a basic rule in the Japanese art of negotiation that "whoever speaks first loses." The same concept can apply in other areas of life as well: Once you've shown someone what you want, it's easier for them to take it away or hold it hostage. Something may be really important to you, but others might just see it as a game . . . and they want to win.

BEYOND THE PUNCH LINE

Of course, there are plenty of times when it's good to reveal things about yourself. But it's also a good idea to know who you're talking to (and who's listening!) before you do—especially at work. Here are some tips to deal with it:

• **Pay attention to the way a "friend" treats other people.** If they're manipulative or insensitive to others' feelings, they'll probably treat you the same way.

• **Do you feel pressured to reveal more about yourself than you want?** If someone's overselling themselves as sympathetic, concerned, or helpful, it might be a warning sign that they have another agenda.

• **Don't be afraid to bail on a relationship.** If you find you've been undermined or taken advantage of because of something you revealed about yourself, don't freak out. Now you know what to expect from that person.

21

Who, Me?

"I want to help the helpless, but I don't
*give a rat's a** about the clueless"*
—Dennis Miller

O ne afternoon, a man decides to take his new sports car for a drive in the country. There's no traffic, so he guns it to seventy mph . . . then eighty . . . then ninety. But as he's turning one particularly sharp corner, he suddenly sees two farmers standing in the road, chatting. Panicked, he cuts the wheel as fast as he can to avoid hitting them but loses control of the car. He hits an embankment, goes flying into the air, and crashes into a field. The farmers watch it all in shock. Finally, one farmer turns to the other and says, "Wow! I guess we got out of the field just in time."

LIFE LESSON

It's frustrating when people who create problems won't take responsibility for the anxiety—or even mayhem—they cause. We all know someone who does that. "They might be friends, family members, or colleagues," writes Dr. Linda Sapadin. "They forget appointments. They're chronically late. They miss deadlines. They expect others to bail them out of whatever trouble they get into." These folks are an annoying fact of life. You can't avoid them completely, but if you're aware that they're out there, you can at least learn to swerve around them when you see them standing in the middle of the road.

BEYOND THE PUNCH LINE

How do you deal with the chronically clueless without becoming their codependent? Here are three options:

1. **Tolerate.** Do nothing . . . because sometimes there's nothing you *can* do. Example: If the clueless troublemaker is a family elder, your boss, or some other authority figure, the best you can do is to let their frustrating behavior roll off your back.

2. **Confront.** On the other hand, if you know the person well, you can try telling them directly how their actions affect you (or others) and how you feel about it. Let them know you're not being judgmental—you're just trying to save a relationship. Your friend might not even be aware of what they're doing. So to illustrate your point, try reviewing a specific situation and discussing how it unfolded.

3. **Avoid.** Then there's the serious possibility that nothing you can do or say will have any effect—except to make you more frustrated. So why bother? Just say, "Excuse me, I have to get going" and walk away. Bonus: Extricating yourself from the situation is also a good way to calm down before frustration takes over.

22

The Old Man and the Cookies

"If you want others to be happy, practice compassion.
If you want to be happy, practice compassion."
—**The Dalai Lama**

An old man was on his deathbed. As he lay there, eyes closed and waiting peacefully for the end, he suddenly got a whiff of his favorite food in the world—fresh-baked chocolate chip cookies! He sniffed again . . . and it was true! His wife was downstairs baking cookies. The aroma suddenly made him feel revitalized. He found the strength to climb out of bed, crawl down the hall, and then hobble down the stairs toward the kitchen—all the time picturing himself eating one last delicious chocolate chip cookie. He finally got to the kitchen and there it was—a platter of cookies on the counter. With his last bit of strength, he crawled across the floor, pulled himself up to the counter, and reached for a cookie. Suddenly he felt the stinging SLAP! of his wife hitting the back of his hand with a metal spatula.

"Don't touch those," she said. "They're for the funeral."

LIFE LESSON

That's no way to treat a dying loved one—or anyone, for that matter. Yet our culture may be headed in that direction. Studies indicate that in the last thirty years, Americans have increasingly lost a sense of empathy—"the ability to understand and share another person's feelings." That's kind of scary, because empathy is considered the basis for meaningful human relationships. It builds trust, cooperation, understanding: all the things that are essential to a healthy society. You can't force other people to be compassionate or understanding, of course. But you can push *yourself* to become more empathetic. And, while you're at it, become a role model for others (see Joke 74).

BEYOND THE PUNCH LINE

Recent research tells us that empathy is actually an attitude: a habit we can develop as part of everyday life. "Empathy doesn't stop developing in childhood," says author Roman Krznaric. "We can nurture its growth throughout our lives—and we can use it as a radical force for social transformation." Some tricks for building empathy in your own life:

1. **Explore your feelings.** Sound a little too woo-woo? It's actually very practical. Being aware of your own feelings is the basis for empathizing with others, yet many of us have learned to suppress our emotions. So try this exercise: At random times during the day, ask yourself, "What am I feeling right now?" and "What if it was me?"

2. **Demonstrate compassion.** When you see someone in distress, say something. Show that you care. It may feel awkward

at first, but keep trying—like a lot of us, you may have to unlearn a lifetime of defensiveness in order to be straightforward and sincere. Another way to show compassion: body language. Lean toward the person; make eye contact; match the tone of your voice to the person's state of mind.

3. **Practice listening.** Suspend judgment. Try to hear what someone is saying from their point of view.

4. **Ask questions.** This is part of listening—a way to increase your knowledge and understanding of others. It also shows a genuine interest in the other person, which inspires trust. To develop a real dialogue, invite them to ask questions of you as well.

5. **Develop your curiosity about people.** Children are naturally curious, but as we get older, we tend to label people rather than wonder about them. Studies suggest that the most empathetic people are also the most curious—so if you want to build empathy, nurture curiosity. One idea: Make it a mission to talk to at least one stranger every week. See what surprising things you can learn about them.

Back to the Front

"Be kind to unkind people. They need it the most."
—Ashleigh Brilliant

I t was the morning of Black Friday, and there was a big sale at the electronics superstore. People had started waiting in line at 5:00 a.m. At about 7:30, there was a huge commotion when a short guy in khaki pants tried working his way to the front of the line. He didn't get very far before the mob grabbed him, wrestled him out of line, and threw him into the parking lot.

The little guy got back up, brushed himself off, and tried again. He was barely able to take another step before an even bigger mob attacked him and threw him out of the line again. Undeterred, the guy got up and started limping toward the line a third time.

"Are you nuts?" asked one of the red-faced mob members. "Don't you know you're just gonna get tossed out of line again?"

"Yeah, I know," the little guy replied. "But if you don't let me get to the front of the line, no one's going to open the store."

LIFE LESSON

You may never be part of a mob, but if you have a hard time controlling your rage, here are two things to remember: First, don't overreact to someone who's cutting in line, talking loudly, driving too fast, and so on. It's not worth bursting a blood vessel simply because someone is acting like a jerk. Second, there might be extenuating circumstances. The loud talker might be speaking to his hard-of-hearing father; the aggressive driver might be trying to get to the hospital. And you never know: Next time, the well-meaning "a**hole" that someone else is cursing out could be you.

BEYOND THE PUNCH LINE

How do you avoid getting angry? Take a deep breath, count to ten, and see if these ideas help:

• **Give your adversary a break.** Your initial reaction may be to take their rude behavior personally, but they may be dealing with other issues—trouble at home, for example. Don't immediately believe the worst about them. All you'll end up doing is adding to your own level of frustration.

• **Repeat the mantra "They're just like me."** We have more in common than we have differences. Remind yourself that the other person loves their family just like you do, wants to be happy just like you do—and makes mistakes just like you do. Despite their rudeness, everyone will be better off if you empathize rather than demonize.

• **Don't be manipulated.** Remember, if you're angry it may be because you've been suckered into it. The other person may actually be trying to provoke a confrontation. Do you want to give them the satisfaction of manipulating you?

• **Look at your own behavior.** We sometimes judge others for things that we do ourselves, or have done. For example, the next time you find yourself yelling at someone while you're driving, ask yourself, "Have I ever driven poorly?" Of course; we all have.

• **Ignore them.** While it may be rude for someone to cut ahead of you in line, is it really that big a deal? Pick your battles: Fight the important ones, but let the rest go. You may think they're *all* important and that ignoring offensive behavior is the same as condoning it. But research shows that people who ignore rude behavior are calmer and better able to focus on the more important tasks that await them.

—— 24 ——

On Second Thought

*"My psychiatrist told me I was crazy, and I said,
'I want a second opinion.' He said, 'Okay, you're ugly too.'"*
—Rodney Dangerfield

A Mafia boss discovers that his bookkeeper has stolen 10 million dollars from him. The bookkeeper is deaf—which is how he got the job in the first place; he would never hear anything that he'd have to testify about in court.

When the boss confronts the bookkeeper about the missing money, he takes along his cousin who knows sign language. The boss says to the cousin, "Ask him where my money is!" Using sign language, the cousin delivers the boss's message.

The bookkeeper signs back, "I don't know what you are talking about."

The cousin tells the Mafia boss, "He says he doesn't know what you're talking about."

The boss pulls out a pistol, puts it to the bookkeeper's head, and says, "Ask him again!"

The cousin signs to the bookkeeper: "If you don't tell him, he'll kill you."

"OK. You win," the bookkeeper signs. "The money is in a suitcase, buried behind my brother-in-law's house!"

The mob boss asks, "What did he say?"

The cousin pauses a moment, then replies, "He says you don't have the guts to pull the trigger."

LIFE LESSON

It's surprising how frequently we take people at their word, even if we don't understand exactly what they're saying. Your doctor says you need treatment for some exotic disease; your accountant says that taking an urban farming deduction is perfectly legal; your lawyer tells you to sign on the dotted line . . . and you just blindly do what they say. What *should* you do? Get a second opinion.

When something's important, it's the cheapest, easiest thing you can do to protect your interests.

BEYOND THE PUNCH LINE

Here's what professionals say about second opinions:

• **You need them more often than you might think.** For example: Statistics show that medical misdiagnoses occur from 10 to 20 percent of the time. Yet polls show that about 70 percent of Americans don't bother to get a second opinion. Even if you're not the victim of bad diagnoses or advice, a second opinion can be useful. There are many different ways to deal with problems. Getting another opinion may be the only way to find the solution that works best for you.

• **A second opinion might not seem warranted at first,** but as a situation progresses, you may find there's something that doesn't seem right and decide you want to consult another professional. It may feel awkward, but don't worry that you're insulting the person you're working with. They should expect and welcome it. "If you have a doctor who would be offended by a second opinion," says Dr. Gregory Abel of the Dana-Farber Cancer Institute, "he or she is probably not the right doctor for you."

• **Make your priorities clear.** Don't assume that your doctor or lawyer knows what's most important to you. Studies show that professionals often have a different focus than their clients.

• **Make sure you ask the right person.** Find a specialist who's dealt with problems like yours. The more experience they have, the more skilled they're likely to be.

It's All in Your Head

"Racism isn't born, folks, it's taught. I have a two-year-old son. You know what he hates? Naps! End of list."
—Dennis Leary

Two cowboys riding across the prairie come upon an Indian lying on his stomach with one ear to the ground. The cowboys stop and one says to the other, "You see that Indian? He's listening to the ground. He can hear things for miles in any direction."

Just then the Indian looks up and says, "Covered wagon. Two miles away. Being pulled by two horses, one brown, one white. Man driving. Inside wagon are woman, child, and household effects."

"That's incredible!" says the other cowboy to his friend. "This Indian knows there's a wagon, how far away it is, how many horses are pulling it, what color they are, who's in the wagon, and even what's in the wagon, all just by listening to the ground!"

The Indian looks up again and says, "Unh-unh. Ran over me about a half hour ago."

Does this joke seem a bit racist? Well, it is. But we had to include at least one joke that addresses the issue of ethnic and racial stereotypes. This one is fairly harmless because it doesn't make fun of anyone. But it does show how biases can influence us without our even knowing it. To the cowboys (and maybe you too) it seems reasonable that a Native American man has his ear to the ground because *everyone knows that Indians are good trackers, and that's how they do it.*

Did you make that assumption? That's the essence of racism and ethnic stereotyping. There doesn't have to be malice or intent—just a set of cartoonish generalizations about a specific group of people. You may never get rid of these assumptions: Some are pretty deeply ingrained. But it's worth trying, because as long as you're seeing people as stereotypes, you're not seeing them as they really are, and you're populating your own world with cartoon characters instead of real human beings.

BEYOND THE PUNCH LINE

Here are three ways you can begin to deal with the ethnic stereotyping already going on in your head:

1. **Get to know your stereotypes.** We've all got them, but most of us are pretty oblivious to the fact they're there. If you observe your first impressions of strangers—the first thoughts that come to mind each time—you'll begin to see the biases clearly. Or try this: Harvard University offers a test to discover your personal biases. It's called "Project Implicit Hidden Bias Test" and you can take it online.

2. **Stop trying to be color-blind.** Think there's something wrong with noticing differences between people? Don't be silly; everyone notices them. But that can be a good thing. Part of the beauty of life is appreciating its variety. Ignoring a person's background might even offend them, especially if their ethnic background is a big part of their identity. So find fulfillment in celebrating the differences between you and others.

3. **Realize that everyone's different.** The sociologist Margaret Mead put it well: "Instead of being presented with stereotypes of age, sex, color, class, or religion, [we all] must have the opportunity to learn that within each range, some people are loathsome and some are delightful." In other words, every group is made up of individuals who are vastly different from one another. Look at the individuals, not the group, and the stereotypes will begin to disappear.

The Perfect Martini

"Have no fear of perfection—you'll never reach it."
—Salvador Dali

A wealthy man goes into a New York City bar that's famous for its world-class cocktails and says to the bartender, "I'd like the world's best martini."

"Well, sir," the bartender replies. "I can make you the world's best martini, but it's going to take a lot of time . . . and it's going to cost you a lot of money."

"Money is no object," says the man.

So the bartender takes the man into the back room, opens a safe, and removes bottles containing the world's rarest gin and the world's rarest vermouth. The man reaches for the bottles and the bartender says, "Patience, sir. Now we must go to Italy."

"Italy?" asks the man.

"Yes, Italy," replies the bartender. So they fly to Florence and then drive to a remote Tuscan hillside where they find the world's most prized olive tree. "Now we'll wait until the olives are perfectly ripe." So they sit down and wait . . . and wait . . . and wait. Days later, the bartender picks two perfect olives and seals them in a hyperbaric chamber.

"When do I get my martini?" asks the man.

"Patience, sir," says the bartender. "For the final step, we must go to San Francisco."

"San Francisco?" asks the man.

"Yes," replies the bartender. So they fly to San Francisco and then take a taxi to a hotel in the Mission District, where they get a luxury suite with a full kitchen so the bartender can *finally* make the martini. "Almost done, sir. We have the perfect gin, the perfect vermouth, and the perfect olives. But the real secret is in how one blends the ingredients. So we must wait again."

"Wait?" the man asks. "For what?"

"An earthquake."

LIFE LESSON

Perfection is an ideal. It's impossible to attain—for mortals, anyway—so "perfectionists" can never be satisfied. They're doomed to a lifetime of finding that nobody and nothing meet their standards. Pretty grim.

So why even bother trying to excel? Because perfection and excellence are entirely different things. Psychological studies show that striving for excellence can lead to success and happiness, while there's a clear correlation between perfectionism and a variety of mental health problems, such as depression and anxiety. The reason: Perfectionists are focused on fear and failure. They're constantly trying to fix what went "wrong," rather than enjoying what went right.

So leave perfectionism to people who just can't help themselves. Do a good job—a great job—the best you can. But be willing to accept "good enough" as a viable result. You'll be happier and more productive.

BEYOND THE PUNCH LINE

Are you a perfectionist, or just highly motivated? Here are some questions that might help you decide whether to pat yourself on the back . . . or contact a therapist at your earliest convenience.

1. **Which of these describes you?**
   a) I did my best, and it's pretty good.
   b) I'll get this right or die trying.

2. **When I take on a project, I'm . . .**
   a) excited and energized.
   b) burdened and afraid I'll fail.

3. **When I complete a project, I'm usually . . .**
   a) satisfied with the work.
   b) disappointed with the mistakes.

4. **My standards are . . .**
   a) high, but reasonable.
   b) high, which makes it hard to finish anything.

5. **Failure is . . .**
   a) sometimes unavoidable.
   b) always unacceptable.

Final thought: "It takes bravery and skill to keep even a very ordinary life going. To persevere through the challenges of love, work, and children is quietly heroic. We should step back to acknowledge in a non-starry-eyed but very real way *that our lives are good enough*—and that this is, in itself, a grand achievement."—*Nikos Marinos*

27

A Monk's Tale

"The squeaking wheel doesn't always get the grease.
Sometimes it gets replaced."
—Serbian proverb

A young man decides to join a Buddhist monastery as a novice and take a vow of silence. He's told that once a year he'll have an interview with the abbot—the head monk—at which time he can say two words. He agrees, and throws himself into monastic life, spending time in deep contemplation and helping fellow monks with their daily tasks.

The first year passes. He's called into the abbot's office and asked what he wants to say. The novice replies: "Work ... hard." The abbot nods and sends him back to the monastery.

Another year passes, and he's called into the abbot's office again. This time, he says, "Floors . . . cold." The abbot nods and sends him back to the monastery.

The third year passes, and again he goes to the abbot's office for an interview. "Well, my son?" the abbot asks. The novice says: "Food . . . bad."

The abbot jumps up and exclaims, "I've heard enough, pack your things and go."

The novice is stunned. "Why?" he says.

"Why?" the abbot responds. "Because you've done nothing but complain since you got here!"

LIFE LESSON

Unfortunately, a little negativity goes a long way. It doesn't take much to create the impression that you're a complainer—and once the listener gets that impression, it's hard to undo. What's more, when you're perceived as a chronic complainer, people are less likely to remember the good things you do or say. It may not be fair, but it's true. People will simply tune you out.

It turns out there's a scientific basis for this reaction. Researchers at Stanford University found that exposure to complaints for thirty minutes a day can actually damage a listener's brain—so maybe people are intuitively just protecting themselves. But that's not all: Recent brain research also indicates that negativity is contagious. According to Trevor Blake in *Three Simple Steps*, "The more we repeat a behavior, the more we become that behavior. . . . Which means that the more you surround yourself with a bunch of complainers, the more likely you are to become a complainer yourself."

BEYOND THE PUNCH LINE

Next time you find yourself itching to say something negative, try taking a breath and pausing before you plow ahead. Imagine how your complaint will sound to your audience; ask yourself how they're likely to respond. Are you really going to change anything—other than people's opinion of you? Because if complaining isn't going to improve things, what's the point? Another reason to avoid it: Studies show that people who complain actually feel *worse* when they're done. They're likely to complain more frequently too, because they're creating neural pathways in their brains that will become the basis of new habits. So apparently, the only thing you can be sure you'll get from complaining is . . . more complaining.

28

The Easy Way

"There are always two choices. Two paths to take.
One is easy . . . and its only reward is that it's easy."
—Anonymous

A guy is walking home from a party one night. Under a streetlight, he sees a man in a tuxedo and a woman in an evening gown crawling around on the side of the road. "Excuse me," he says, "what on earth are you doing?"

The woman looks up at him mournfully and says, "I lost my diamond ring!"

"That's terrible," he says. "Let me help you look for it." So he gets down on his hands and knees and starts looking. He carefully scans every inch of the street, the curb, and the sidewalk, and after about thirty minutes, he's sure they've covered the entire area. "I'm sorry, ma'am, but we've looked everywhere and there's just no sign of the ring. Are you sure you lost it here?"

"Oh, no," she says, pointing to the other side of the street. "I lost it over there."

The guy can't believe it. "Then why are you looking *here*?" he asks.

"Well," she answers, "the light's better."

LIFE LESSON

Searching for what you really want in life is a big commitment. There's no guarantee you'll find it, even if you look in the most promising places. But if you're looking where you *know* you won't find it, you're just wasting precious time. Sure, it may be more comfortable to hang out where "the light's better" and the searching is easier. But in the end, you won't get what you're looking for. It's your choice: Go for comfort . . . or fulfillment.

BEYOND THE PUNCH LINE

Are you looking in the right place? At some level, you already know the answer. But if you're having a hard time figuring it out, you may need to practice listening to your intuition—your "inner voice." Surprisingly, this really is something you can practice. Scientific evidence suggests that the more you try to hear that voice, the better you get at it. "It's all about learning to use unconscious information in your brain," explains one researcher.

Want to start an "inner dialogue"? Here are some guided questions to ask yourself:

• Do you enjoy what you're doing? How about where you're doing it?

• If you had a year to live, what would you do?

• Does it feel like you're growing?

• Do you always wind up in the same situation?

• Are you making uncomfortable compromises?

• Are you only doing it because it's safe and easy?

If you're not hearing your inner voice, try listening to your body. Chronic physical ailments like insomnia, anxiety, and stress are sometimes connected to internal conflict. If you're not feeling healthy, passionate, or joyful about your life, your body might be telling you that it's time to look for fulfillment in a new place.

—— 29 ——

Hello, I Must Be Going

"Nothing makes one feel so strong as a call for help."
—Pope Paul VI

A guy goes into a psychiatrist's office. "What seems to be the problem?" asks the doctor.

"I have difficulty making friends," the man replies. "Can you help me, you fat ugly bastard?"

LIFE LESSON

Sometimes we find ourselves pushing away the very people we're counting on for assistance. The reason: We're ambivalent about getting help, because it feels like an admission of failure or weakness. But it's not. Asking for help is actually a sign of strength—an indication that we're ready to face our demons and conquer them.

So don't give in to the nagging voice in your head that says you *should* be able to do things on your own. Instead, trust the other voice—the one telling you how smart you are for enlisting someone else's aid. Then push your excuses aside and get the help you need.

BEYOND THE PUNCH LINE

Experts say that one reason many of us have a hard time asking for help is that we've never learned how to do it properly. Here are five practical suggestions that might make it easier:

1. **Redefine your quest as something positive.** You're not a beggar—you're someone who wants to improve your life. You're not asking for help—you're looking for support. Don't feel weak for asking—celebrate your good fortune that you don't have to do it alone.

2. **Be creative about who you ask.** Are there people in your world who have experience dealing with your issues? Example: If you're trying to master your smartphone, is there a teenager who'd be willing to help? If you're dealing with a medical procedure, do you know of someone who's already been through it?

3. **If it's hard to take the big step and actually ask, try thinking of your request as an invitation, not an imposition.** Studies show that you'll probably find assistance sooner than you expect, because people like to help. And if you express your gratitude freely, it may even help create a closer relationship.

4. **Ask in person.** And when you do, be specific about what you need. That will make it easier for whomever you're asking to understand what's being asked. You can also evaluate whether they can legitimately be of assistance.

5. **Present your problem in a way that allows the helper some "ownership" of it.** That is, make them feel they have a stake in your success. For example, if you treat them as experts and make it clear that you know your success depends on their knowledge, they're more likely to take a personal interest and stick with you to the end.

———— 30 ————

Anchors Aweigh!

"The basic tool for the manipulation of reality is the manipulation of words."
—Philip K. Dick

A grizzled old sea captain decided to test one of his recent recruits. "Let's say you see a storm heading your way off the starboard side. What would you do?"

"I would throw out an anchor, sir," said the deckhand confidently.

"All right," said the captain. "Then let's say a second storm was coming in from your port side. Then what would you do?"

The deckhand answered, "I'd throw out another anchor, Captain."

"But what if another storm was coming in on your bow?"

"Throw out another anchor, Captain!"

"Look behind you!" yelled the captain, "Now there's a fourth storm coming up from the aft! What would you do?"

"Throw out another anchor, sir!"

"Wait a minute," said the captain. "Exactly where are you getting all these anchors from?"

"The same place you're getting all those storms from, sir."

LIFE LESSON

Every conversation has a frame—the assumptions and point of view that define it. In this joke, the captain frames the conversation as a challenge to the sailor's knowledge—but the sailor fights back by reframing it as a ridiculous scenario. The lesson: Whoever controls the frame controls the conversation. It's a skill anyone can develop—and if you learn to do it well, no one will even notice it's happening.

BEYOND THE PUNCH LINE

The goal in framing a conversation isn't to dominate it. It's the opposite—because framing only works if the other people are fully engaged in the discussion, expressing their own ideas. You merely want to direct the conversation so people are thinking about a topic *you* choose. You're the navigator; steer the conversation where you want it to go—and when it wanders off course, gently guide it back. Here are a few ways to do that:

1. **Ask questions.** When you're asking questions, you're picking the topic, and the other person is responding to your

thoughts. Science shows that when people are talking about themselves and what they think, it stimulates a pleasure center of the brain . . . so even though you're leading them, they'll feel good about it. Give them lots of time to talk.

2. **Validate.** If someone goes off-topic or tries to change the frame, you can retake control by validating what they've said—and at the same time, guiding them back into the conversation you want to have: "That's a good point, but how do you think it would work with . . ." This shows respect and keeps them engaged, but gives you the upper hand. Key point: Don't argue with them—guide them.

3. **Pay attention.** If it feels as though someone's uncomfortable with the topic or direction of the discussion, ask them directly and encourage them to share their thoughts; then offer support. Even if the point is a small one, unless it's dealt with, it can keep others from fully participating. Plus you'll be winning their confidence by demonstrating that you care. If the other person becomes aggressive, don't respond in kind; stay steady and unflappable.

4. **Use their language.** Listen for the terms or phrases the person uses frequently—and employ them strategically. This creates a sense of connection and enables you to reach directly into their internal thought process.

31

Nonverbal Communication

"It's a rather rude gesture,
but at least it's clear what you mean."
—Katharine Hepburn

An elderly man and woman are sitting on a bench in a nursing home. The man says, "You know, I forget how old I am."

"Don't worry," says the woman. "I can tell you how old you are. Just take off your clothes and bend over."

The guy is puzzled by this, but takes off his clothes and bends over. The woman looks him up and down, and says, "OK, you're eighty-three."

The man is amazed. "Really? How can you tell?" he asks.

The woman says, "You told me yesterday."

LIFE LESSON

Think you're a mystery to other people? Guess again. People almost always know more about you than you realize. It may be because you've absentmindedly forgotten what you told them yesterday. But more likely, it's because of nonverbal communication. The people you interact with are constantly observing your speech patterns, facial expressions, gestures, body language, etc., looking for clues about who you are. (Don't get paranoid—you do it too.)

You don't have to do anything with this info. Just be aware that the real you is on display for anyone who's really paying attention. And if you're wondering whether to be honest with someone about something that's going on for you . . . well, don't be surprised if they already know.

BEYOND THE PUNCH LINE
Here are four ways we "talk" to other people without realizing it:

1. **Body language.** According to researchers, body language has evolved over millions of years, and it's largely the same all over the world. Shuffling feet or slouching posture means a lack of self-confidence. Raised elbows is a sign of distress. Narrowed eyes and a lowered chin indicate anger. A tilted head can be a sign of curiosity or a sign of flirting, and so on.

2. **Gestures.** They're often cultural, but some are universal. We instinctively know, for instance, that a person extending their hands toward us with palms facing up is communicating honesty. A hand over the mouth is a sign of apprehension. And touching the *suprasternal notch* (the dimple above the sternum, where the neck meets the collarbone) is an expression of anxiety or defensiveness.

3. **Microexpressions.** These barely perceptible facial movements occur in as little as $1/25$ of a second. We register them subconsciously—which may be how we "sense" when a person's not being 100 percent honest. For example, you may appear calm, but if the muscles around your mouth are slightly pulled back and your eyebrows are raised, *for just a*

fraction of a second, others can perceive that something's not right—specifically, that you're afraid or lying. Scientists speculate we express seven different emotions this way—disgust, anger, fear, sadness, happiness, surprise, and contempt—and they're extremely hard to fake.

4. **Mirroring.** If we feel connected to someone, we unconsciously respond with expressions and body language similar to theirs. If you smile, I might smile. If you've got your hand on your side, I might do that too. Sometimes it's like "monkey see, monkey do"—people imitate each other exactly. Other times it's more subtle—people lean in the same direction or gesture with the same hand. A lack of reciprocal behavior is also significant: It indicates emotional distance. If someone isn't mirroring us, it's like announcing that they're not engaged by the interaction and maybe don't approve of us.

32

The Whole Truth

"There are no whole truths; all truths are half-truths."
—Alfred North Whitehead

O ut at sea, a young deckhand named Charlie drank alcohol for the first time in his life, and he got pretty sloppy. The next day, he saw that in the ship's official log, the captain had entered: "Charlie was drunk today."

Charlie went to the captain and asked him to make an additional entry noting that it was his first time drinking. "Otherwise," he explained, "it looks like this is a common occurrence for me, which it definitely is not!"

"That's too bad," said the captain, "but the entry was truthful, and therefore it will not be changed."

A few days later, when it was Charlie's job to write the log, he entered, "The captain was sober today."

LIFE LESSON
Just because something is true doesn't mean it's accurate . . . or that it tells the whole story.

BEYOND THE PUNCH LINE
Trying to mislead people with truthful statements is called *paltering*. People do it routinely, and a Harvard study shows

that even though it's dishonest, we still tend to consider it more acceptable than outright lying. Here are five of the most common ways that people "palter":

1. **Cherry picking.** They select a few facts that support their point and ignore any that contradict it, then present the data as if it were definitive proof. This sounds convincing to listeners— who are rarely familiar enough with the details to challenge it.

2. **Misdirection.** They tell the truth, but avoid answering the question. For example, in the Harvard study, participants were told to sell a used car that had significant mechanical problems. They were given the option of being completely honest, but 71 percent still chose to deliver this misdirecting line: "The car drives smoothly and is very responsive. Just last week it started up with no problems when the temperature was -5 degrees Fahrenheit." True? Yes, but also seriously misleading.

3. **Exaggeration.** They make small differences seem like big ones. If you say it with enough emphasis, listeners will apparently accept the idea, for example, that a 1-percent drop (or rise) in participation (or anything) is *shocking*. Politicians do this all the time.

4. **Anecdotes.** Facts don't support your claim? No problem: Instead of employing data, tell a story; use someone's experience to "prove" your point. Of course, one person's experience doesn't prove anything, but anecdotal information is still convincing to many listeners.

5. **Phony averages.** Suppose, for example, there are eleven salaried employees at a company. Ten make $10,000 a year; the

eleventh is the owner . . . who makes $500,000. The average salary at that company is $54,000. True or false?

Ironically, while the Harvard study shows that the average person feels their own paltering is more ethically acceptable than lying, it also shows that when people discover one of their peers has paltered, "they're less likely to trust that person in the future." The lesson: Deep down, we all recognize that paltering is lying.

— 33 —

Do the Right Thing

"I have my values, and if you don't like them,
well, I've got some others."
—Mark Twain

 ten-year-old boy was questioning his father about being a good businessman. "Daddy," he asked, "what are ethics?"

"Well, it's like this, son," answered his father. "You know how your uncle Jim and I own a store together?"

"Uh-huh."

"Well, let's say a customer comes in and buys a fifty-dollar hat but accidentally overpays for it by twenty bucks. If I split the difference with Jim, that's ethics."

LIFE LESSON

It's a common mistake, especially for younger people, to assume that just because something seems clearly right or wrong to you, other people share—or even respect—your point of view. That's no excuse for bad behavior; it's just a reality. Example: The TV mobsters on *The Sopranos* thought it was ethical to kill someone who'd betrayed them. Was their code of ethics the same as yours? No (we hope), but it was real to them. Everyone has their own definition of "moral" behavior. Be prepared to encounter people whose moral compass is set differently from yours.

BEYOND THE PUNCH LINE

The dictionary defines ethics as "the set of rules that determine whether an individual or group's actions are right or wrong." So if you want to know what someone is likely to do in any given situation, examine their ethics. It's like reading the rulebook to their lives. But don't expect it to be an easy study—people's belief systems can be really complicated. For example, a person may feel it's okay to steal from strangers, but not from friends. Lie to a boss, but not to a wife. Cheat on a test, but not in sports. Deciphering these contradictions can be challenging, but remember:

• **Don't let your own values get in the way of seeing someone else's clearly.** It's a paradox that our values seem absolute to us when, in fact, they're highly personal.

• **Each person has a set of ethics that guides them,** and as long as there's an internal logic, they probably don't care whether their rules make sense to you (or anyone else, for that matter).

• You don't have to agree with, or approve of, other people's ethics. But if you're unable to understand and accept them as they are, you'll find yourself at a disadvantage in business, politics, and all social interaction.

34

Bring in the "B" Team

"If you don't have a plan B, you don't have a plan."
—Adam Bryant

One morning, a man looks out of his bedroom window and sees an enormous grizzly bear in a tree. So he looks in the yellow pages and sure enough, there's an ad for Bob's Bear Removal. He calls the number, and twenty minutes later Bob shows up at his door. "Thank goodness you're here," says the man. He takes Bob to the backyard and, pointing to the grizzly, asks, "Can you help me?"

"Absolutely," Bob tells him, "but I'll need your help . . . and some special supplies." A few minutes later he returns from his truck with a ladder, a baseball bat, a leash, a German shepherd, and a shotgun. "Listen carefully," he says. "I'm going to use the ladder to climb up the tree, and then I'm going to whack the bear with the bat. You stay here and hold my German shepherd securely on the leash. The moment I swing the bat, release the dog. He's been specially trained to do one thing and one thing only: wrap his teeth around the bear's genitals and not let go until the animal is completely subdued. You got all that?"

"Sure," replies the man. "But what's the shotgun for?"

"Oh, that's plan B. If the bear ends up knocking *me* out of the tree, shoot the dog."

LIFE LESSON

Let's be realistic. There's no chance that *all* your projects are going to work out as anticipated (see Joke 63). And what happens when one of them doesn't?

If you're prepared with a contingency plan—a plan B—you've already shifted the odds in your favor. So don't wait until you're in trouble. Having a plan B ready—and maybe a plan C and a plan D too—will not only increase your chances for success, it will give you more confidence, reduce stress, and enable you to be more flexible and creative as events unfold.

BEYOND THE PUNCH LINE

Experts recommend creating plan B at the same time you create plan A. Here's why:

1. Once you start on a project, you probably won't have the time—or the inclination—to focus on planning again. Trying to keep up with deadlines and dealing with current problems will take all your attention.

2. It's easier to overcome resistance at the beginning. "People are often poorly motivated to develop a strong 'Plan B' because they have so much of an emotional investment in 'Plan A,'" writes a risk management expert. Result: "It gets stuck at the bottom of their to-do lists as a task that never gets done."

3. You're less likely to forget important details in the early stages of planning . . . and since you're probably evaluating alternatives anyway, that's a good time to pick your two favorites and call them plan A and plan B.

4. It's smart to determine the "trigger"—the event or circumstance that will tell you it's time for plan B—*before* you plunge in. And while you're considering that, you can figure out *how* you'll transition to plan B if necessary.

5. It's a chance to bring more people into the process. "You can't take on an entire project alone and expect it to go well," insists a prominent corporate CEO, explaining that if you do it right, you won't "just have a Plan B, you'll have other people readily available to help you execute it when the time comes."

35

Head Case

"Vilify, vilify, some of it will always stick."
—Pierre Beaumarchais

O n her way to work every day, a woman walks past a pet shop. One day there's a parrot in the window. As she stops to admire the bird, it says, "Hey, lady! You're ugly." Stunned, the woman looks around, and the parrot says, "Yeah, I'm talking to you. Beat it, will you? You're scaring the puppies!" Furious, the woman storms away.

The next day, as she passes the shop, the parrot says, "Wow! Lady, you are *really* ugly!" This continues for days, and finally the woman can't stand it anymore. She marches into the pet shop and tells the owner that if that parrot calls her ugly one more time, she'll have the man charged with harassment and sue him for every cent he's got. "I'm so sorry, ma'am. I promise he'll never do it again."

The next day, as she passes the shop, the parrot says, "Hey, lady." The woman stops in her tracks, turns, and stares intently at the bird. The parrot climbs onto its perch and starts swinging gently, then looks away from the woman and says, "You know."

LIFE LESSON

Anyone can get into your head if they want to. All they have to do is keep repeating their message, and eventually you'll internalize it. This isn't speculation—scientific studies have proven that after being exposed to a message enough times, our brains begin to process it as if we had thought of it ourselves.

But wait, there's more. Science has also proven that humans have an innate *negative bias*—which means that we're generally inclined to pay more attention to negative ideas than positive ones. When you put these two traits together, you can see how easy it is for narcissistic bullies to be abusive with words. They bombard us with negative messages and pretty soon we're doing their work for them, saying the same negative things to ourselves.

You can't stop people from trying to influence your thinking this way, but you can recognize a power play when you see it and learn to deflect their controlling behavior. Your best defense is to learn their strategies, and then observe what happens when they try to use them . . . or for that matter, when *you* do. (Own up. We all do it sometimes.)

BEYOND THE PUNCH LINE

In her book *The Verbally Abusive Relationship*, Patricia Evans lists a number of ways that verbal bullies try to influence the way we think about ourselves. Here are five examples to look out for:

1. **Countering.** No matter what you say, even if you're just expressing a personal preference, they'll counter with the opposite point of view. It's not just arguing—it's a dismissive attack.

2. **Blocking and diverting.** Have you got a point to make? They'll alter the conversation to keep you from making it . . . or just ignore you altogether.

3. **Trivializing.** This is a passive-aggressive attack on your self-esteem. Evans says: "[It] makes light of your work, your efforts, your interests, or your concerns. It is done very covertly, often with feigned innocence." For example, they might "innocently" deflate your pride in an accomplishment by saying something like, "But haven't you been working on that for a long time?"

4. **Discounting.** This makes you question the validity of your own thoughts, feelings, or experiences. For example: You tell someone that something they did hurt your feelings, and they discount it with "You're just too sensitive."

5. **Judging and criticizing.** There's nothing subtle about this approach—it's an outright attack, often starting with the word "You." Evans says: "Most 'you' statements are judgmental, critical, and abusive," as in: "You're never satisfied" or "You're really defensive" or (if a parrot is talking to you) "You're really ugly."

36

Elementary

*"Sometimes the questions are complicated
and the answers are simple."*
—Dr. Seuss

Sherlock Holmes and Dr. Watson go on a camping trip. After a good dinner and a bottle of wine, they retire for the night and go to sleep. Some hours later, Holmes wakes up and nudges his faithful friend. "Watson, look up at the sky and tell me what you see."

"I see millions and millions of stars, Holmes," replies Watson.

"And what do you deduce from that?"

Watson ponders for a minute. "Well, astronomically, it tells me that there are millions of galaxies and potentially billions of planets. Astrologically, I observe that Saturn is in Leo. Meteorologically, I suspect that we will have a beautiful day tomorrow. Theologically, I can see that God is all powerful, and that we are a small and insignificant part of the universe. But what does it tell you, Holmes?"

Holmes is silent for a moment. "Watson, you idiot!" he says. "Someone has stolen our tent!"

LIFE LESSON

When you overthink a situation, it's easy to miss what's right in front of you. The problem you're facing *might* require complex analysis, but doesn't it make sense to look for the obvious solution first? That's especially true if the situation requires action. We can get caught up in what experts call *analysis paralysis*—an inability to make decisions because we're focused on trying to see every side of an issue. The result: We often lose sight of not only the obvious answer but of the original question as well.

BEYOND THE PUNCH LINE

A few easy tricks to keep from overthinking things:

• **Don't be afraid to ask "stupid" questions—especially if people are using jargon or technical language.** It's easy to miss the obvious and go off on a tangent when you don't really understand the problem.

• **Pay attention to context.** A problem doesn't exist in a vacuum. Seeing it in context will reduce the possibility of expanding it to universe-sized proportions and will help you keep it small and manageable.

• **Try to filter out your own assumptions.** "The more infatuated I am with my own brilliance," says one observer, "the more likely I am to ignore the obvious." His strategy: "I describe my solution to a disinterested third party whom I trust. Before I've finished I'll usually discover the obvious, modify my solution, or . . . just say, 'Never mind.'"

37

Life Is a Beach

"If the only prayer you said in your whole life
was 'thank you,' that would suffice."
—Meister Eckhart

An old lady is watching her grandchild playing on the beach when a huge wave suddenly comes in and sweeps him out to sea. Frantic, she falls down on her knees and pleads, "Please God, save my only grandson. Please, I beg of you, bring him back." Suddenly, another wave comes in and delivers the boy back onto the beach, good as new.

The old lady looks up to heaven and says: "He had a hat!"

LIFE LESSON

Have you ever noticed that no matter how much we get, we always seem to want a little more? That's human nature. Ironically, studies have shown that experiencing gratitude for what we already have actually makes us happier than getting more. So the next time something good happens to you, why not take the opportunity to reflect on how lucky you are . . . and say thank you.

BEYOND THE PUNCH LINE

When we take time to express gratitude, we actually feel better both mentally and physically. Gratitude can help you . . .

• **Sleep better.** According to the *Journal of Applied Psychology*, a 2011 study showed that people who took fifteen minutes at bedtime to write down their thoughts in a "gratitude journal" reported experiencing better sleep than people who didn't.

• **Feel better.** A 2012 study found that people who reported feeling gratitude about their lives also reported having fewer aches and pains than people who did not. Other studies have found that gratitude reduces negative feelings such as jealousy, resentment, and depression, while increasing a sense of well-being.

• **Make *other* people feel better.** A study published in *Psychological Science* revealed that people with a greater sense of gratitude about their lives were more likely to offer assistance to others, which increased both their own happiness and that of the people they were helping.

And here's a how-to tip from Harvard Medical School: "Write a thank-you note to someone, expressing your enjoyment and appreciation of that person's impact on your life. Send it, or better yet, deliver and read it in person if possible. Make a habit of sending at least one gratitude letter a month. Once in a while, write one to yourself."

38

Just Do It

"There is only one thing more painful than learning from experience, and that is not learning from experience."
—Laurence J. Peter

Two boys are walking through the woods one day when they spy some rabbit turds. One of the boys says, "Hey, what are those things?"

"They're smart pills," says his friend. "Eat them and they'll make you smarter."

So the first boy eats them and says, "Ecch . . . these taste like crap."

"See?" the other boy replies. "You're getting smarter already."

LIFE LESSON

We're all looking for an easy path to wisdom. (Hey—you're reading this book, aren't you?) Unfortunately, there's no such thing as "smart pills." What *does* make you smarter is learning from experience. Of course, like the kid in the joke, you don't always learn the easy way; some lessons can be pretty distasteful. But the good news is that if you really learn them, you never forget them . . . and you won't have to spend the rest of your life confusing rabbit turds with smart pills.

BEYOND THE PUNCH LINE

We don't need anyone telling us how to learn from experience. But a theory proposed in the 1970s by psychologist David Kolb may help us understand and control the process.

Kolb suggests that learning from experience is a four-part process: We don't just learn from doing, but also from reflecting on what we've done, thinking about what might work better (or what works well) for us, and testing our new ideas to see if they make sense. Then the whole process starts again. Kolb calls it a Learning Cycle (see the diagram below).

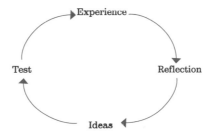

One of the more interesting parts of this theory: It recognizes that we all have different modes of learning, depending on the situation. "Because of our hereditary equipment, our . . . life experiences, and the demands of our environment," says Kolb, "we [each] develop a preferred way of learning." So in his view, experiential learning doesn't necessarily start with the experience—it can start anywhere in the cycle. Let's say you want to paint a house. You might start learning by watching a house painter and reflecting on what you see; or you might start by reading a book about house painting and getting ideas about best practices; or you might just get a can of paint and start slapping paint on the house. Once the cycle is started, you're learning in a way that works for you.

39

Hidden Agenda

"Men who call just to say hello
generally have ulterior motives."
—Stieg Larsson

An old guy goes into a confessional and says to the priest, "Father, I'm eighty years old and I've been married for fifty years, but I think I've done a bad thing. Last night I went home with two beautiful twenty-year-old women and made love to them all night long."

The priest ponders the situation and then says, "When did you last go to confession, my son?"

"Never," says the old guy. "I'm Jewish."

"Then why are you telling me this?" asks the priest.

"Are you kidding?" the man says. "I'm telling everyone."

LIFE LESSON

Like the old guy in the joke, everyone has their own agenda. There's nothing wrong with that; the problem comes when people like him hide their motives and try to hijack *your* agenda for their benefit. Dealing with other people's hidden agendas is a frustrating waste of time . . . and more important, it can prevent you from accomplishing your own goals. So if you feel that someone's manipulating you, avoid them. If you can't avoid them, just deal with them as quickly as possible and move on. After all, who needs the grief?

BEYOND THE PUNCH LINE

How can you tell when someone has a hidden agenda? It starts with the feeling that something's not quite right. When that little voice speaks, pay attention. Look a little closer at:

• **Body language.** It reveals a lot about our unspoken thoughts. Does someone avoid eye contact when you ask a direct question? Are their arms crossed? Are they leaning away from you? Do they blink a lot when they're speaking? All of these could be signs that they're hiding something or not telling the whole truth.

• **Hand gestures.** People use forceful hand gestures to emphasize a point and gentle gestures to show they care. Watch what they're doing with their hands—is it congruent with what they're saying? If not, there could be an unspoken motive.

• **Tone of voice.** Does it complement the message? Too loud? Too soft? Speaking too fast? Listen for signs of anger

• **The topic of conversation.** You try to talk about the weather, and they keep returning to the fact that they need someone to sit with Grandma this Saturday. If the conversation always seems to circle back to them and what they need, it's clear they have their own agenda.

40

Who's in Charge Here?

*"If a black cat crosses your path,
it signifies that the animal is going somewhere."*
—Groucho Marx

A man sees his friend on the street and asks, "Hey, what's wrong? You look kind of down." His friend sighs. "Yeah. I really thought today was going to be my day. I woke up at exactly 7:00 a.m. and realized it was July 7—the seventh day of the seventh month. Then I put on my pants and found exactly seven dollars in my pocket. I knew *it must be a sign*! So I took the number 7 bus to the racetrack and—would you believe it—the seventh horse in the seventh race was named Seven-Up ... running at 7-to-1 odds! So I bet seven hundred dollars on him."

"What happened?" asked the friend.

"He came in seventh."

LIFE LESSON

It *should* go without saying that taking cues from "signs" and fortune cookies is an undependable way to get control of your life. But sometimes we do it anyway. Mostly that just amounts to harmless diversion, but people sometimes lose perspective and really start to believe it. That's when you need a reality check. It's fun to think the universe is delivering a secret message directly to you . . . but in the end, you're the one making the decision and you're the one who has to live with the consequences.

BEYOND THE PUNCH LINE

In recent polls, more than 50 percent of Americans say they're "at least a little superstitious." Experts attribute this to our innate need to control events in our lives. "Superstitions provide people with the sense that they've done one more thing to try to ensure the outcome they are looking for," says psychologist Stuart Vyse. That tendency can work to your advantage, but it's also an indication that you're looking outside yourself for affirmation.

Psychologists use the term *external locus of control* to describe this trait. People with an *internal locus of control* believe they're "in charge of the events that occur in their life." But those with an external locus of control believe that "chance, fate, or outside forces determine life events." Studies show that people with an internal locus of control are generally happier and able to accomplish more. According to a University of Michigan nationwide survey, Americans who said they felt "in control of their lives" also had "extraordinarily positive feelings of happiness."

The good news is that psychologists say our locus of control is mostly learned behavior. So if you want to develop your internal locus of control, you can . . . and it's easier than you think. The trick is to take control of your life slowly, with small, simple changes. Once you have those mastered, you can move on to bigger things.

41

That's News to Me

*"We all have a blind spot,
and it's shaped exactly like us."*
—Junot Diaz

An elderly woman goes to the doctor and tells him she has a problem with frequent gas. "Fortunately," she says, "my farts never smell and they're always silent. As a matter of fact, I've farted at least ten times since I've been here, and I'll bet you didn't even notice!"

"I see," the doctor says, handing her a vial of pills. "I'd like you to take one of these every day. Then come back and see me next week."

The following week the old lady returns. "Doctor," she says, "I don't know *what* you gave me, but since I started taking those pills, my silent farts stink like hell."

The doctor says, "Good! Now that we've cleared up your sinuses, let's work on your hearing."

LIFE LESSON

It's amusing that the woman can be so sure and so wrong at the same time. Clearly, everyone knows something about her that she doesn't know about herself. But isn't that true about all of us? We all have blind spots about our limitations. In some ways, they're worse than the limitations themselves, because if you need to change something in your life but you can't see it, then you also can't do anything about it. So if something's not working for you, try looking for the blind spot first.

BEYOND THE PUNCH LINE

If you're aware of a problem already, it's not a blind spot—at least not anymore. Blind spots are the problems you don't realize you have. Here are some tips to help you see them:

• Notice how people react to you. Are they expressing disdain? Envy? Caring? Frustration? Affection? Those reactions are telling you something about yourself—especially if they're consistent from person to person.

• Listen to the way people describe you. Does it fit with your self-image? Sociologist Martha Beck has suggested these fill-in-the-blank sentences to help identify a blind spot:
  • "People always tell me that I'm _____."
  • "People compliment me about _____."
  • "When people are angry with me, they say that _____."
  • "I often get thanked for _____."

If your answers are in line with your self-image, congratulations. If not . . . Blind Spots!

• Cultivate friendships with people from diverse backgrounds. Some blind spots are common among people with the same cultural or socioeconomic origins. Exposing yourself to different cultures, backgrounds, and points of view will help to bring these blind spots out into the open.

42

Dead Weight

"We are all faced with a series of great opportunities
brilliantly disguised as impossible situations."
—Charles Swindoll

A young man from the big city moved to the country and bought a donkey from a local farmer for two hundred dollars. The farmer took the money and said he'd deliver the donkey the next day.

The next afternoon, the farmer arrived at the man's house . . . with an empty truck. "Sorry, mister. I have some bad news," the farmer said. "The donkey died."

"Well," said the man, "so just give me back my two hundred dollars."

"Sorry, mister," the farmer replied. "I can't give it back—I already spent it."

The man thought for a moment and said, "Okay, then give me the dead donkey."

"What are you going to do with it?" the farmer asked.

"I'm going to raffle her off," said the man.

"You can't raffle off a dead donkey," exclaimed the farmer.

"Sure I can," the man calmly replied. "I just won't tell anyone she's dead."

A few weeks later the farmer happened to run into the young man and asked what happened with the dead donkey. "I raffled her off," he told the farmer. "I sold three hundred tickets at $2.50 apiece and made a profit of $547.50."

Stunned, the farmer said, "Wow! Didn't anyone complain?"

"Just the guy who won," said the man. "So I gave him back his $2.50."

LIFE LESSON

What the guy in the joke did is unethical and probably illegal, but you can't help but be impressed by his ability to turn lemons into lemonade—that is, turn a bad situation into a fruitful opportunity. Faced with a tough situation, we all have a tendency to say, "That's it! I'm screwed!" But, as the guy demonstrated, there's an alternative. Instead of quitting, take a moment to let panic subside, and give yourself a chance to adjust to the new circumstances. Then channel your creativity and see what ideas come up. Do that a few times, and it will start to become second nature. You'll be surprised by your ingenuity; you'll be gratified by your success.

BEYOND THE PUNCH LINE

How can you approach an overwhelming situation in a way that makes it work for you? Here are a few tips:

1. **Remember you've been there before.** At some point you've had to overcome tough situations and find ways to turn them to your advantage—*everyone* has. Don't discount those experiences. Empower yourself with your own success stories.

2. **Shift your perception.** Find a different way to look at your situation (see Joke 30). It may not be what you wanted or expected, but don't get stuck there. Find an aspect you can work with. It's probably staring you in the face; you just have to see it.

3. **Be proactive.** Survey the situation and identify something you can take control of. Research shows that the feeling of being in control (even in a small way) engenders optimism—a key element to successfully bouncing back from a potential setback.

4. **Look for the lesson.** Transform a difficult experience into personal growth. You can't change what happened, but you can always learn something from it . . . which helps build optimism. And, as one friend of ours says, "You can confidently leave this situation knowing that you will make a wiser, more informed decision down the road."

43

Value Meal

*"I wonder how much it would take to buy a soap bubble,
if there were only one in the world."*
—Mark Twain

Walking through an art gallery, a man notices two similar still-life paintings. Both show a table covered by a red-and-white checked cloth. Sitting on the table is a bottle of wine, a loaf of bread, and a wheel of cheese. One painting is priced at a thousand dollars, and the other is fifteen hundred. The man looks carefully at both but can't tell the difference. Finally, he goes over to the gallery owner. "I don't get it," he says. "Why is that painting so much more expensive than the other one?" The gallery owner smiles, points to the more expensive painting, and says, "That one has imported cheese."

LIFE LESSON

Next time you're trying to decide whether something is worth the price, ask yourself if the promised value is real, or just "imported cheese." People may tell you something is a bargain because they want to sell it, but there's really no universal standard of value. What matters is what it's worth to you.

To prove our point, take this mini-quiz. What would you pay for:

1. A piece of Justin Timberlake's half-eaten French toast?

2. A pink Hot Wheels car called the "Beatnik Bandit"?

3. A Kellogg's corn flake shaped like the state of Illinois?

You probably answered a dollar ... or less. But here's what people actually did pay for them: 1. $1,025; 2. $15,250; 3. $1,350.

44

You're the Bomb

"If one looks with a cold eye at the mess man has made of history, it is difficult to avoid the conclusion that he has been afflicted by some built-in mental disorder which drives him towards self-destruction."
—Arthur Koestler

Hovering above Earth in their flying saucers, two alien life-forms are talking to each other. The first one says, "I've been observing the dominant life-forms on this planet. It appears they have developed satellite-based nuclear weaponry."

"Fascinating," the second one replies. "Are they an emerging intelligence?"

"I don't think so," says the first one. "They have them aimed at themselves."

LIFE LESSON

We earthlings tend to overlook some of our dumbest, most self-destructive behaviors (SDBs) and even think they're normal. It just seems to be part of our nature. In fact, we've all probably got some fully weaponized SDBs aimed at our own heads right now. We may not be able to eliminate them, but we can at least be aware of them . . . and that's the first step toward negotiating a "meaningful truce."

BEYOND THE PUNCH LINE

Want to know where you've stashed the hidden SDBs in your life? Try examining the clues that can tell you where to look. Five prime candidates to check out:

1. **Your friends.** Are they supportive people who make your life better, or are they jealous, competitive, manipulative? If they're harming instead of helping you . . . SDB alert.

2. **Your stress.** Do you think of stress as a symbol of pride instead of a self-inflicted attack on your health? And do you refuse to ask other people for help? Bull's-eye.

3. **Your decision making.** Everyone second-guesses themselves at some point, but if you're letting second-guessing turn into an inability to make decisions at all, call the bomb squad.

4. **Your attitude.** There's nothing wrong with acknowledging shortcomings, but if you're obsessive about it and can't let go, your finger's on the trigger.

5. **Your fears.** If you avoid taking chances because you're afraid of failing, you're probably stunting your emotional growth. Being risk-averse might feel safe, but if it feels extreme, you've found something explosive.

Note: Don't panic if you recognize yourself in any of these behaviors. It just means that you've found your SDBs. Now you can start to change them (see Joke 1).

—— 45 ——

The Naked Wife

"The right man is the one who seizes the moment."
—Johann Wolfgang von Goethe

A man steps into the shower right after his wife has finished her shower. Just then, the doorbell rings. So the wife quickly wraps a towel around herself and goes to answer the door. She opens the door to find her next-door neighbor, Mark, standing there. Before she can say a word, he says, "I'll give you three hundred dollars if you drop that towel." She thinks for a second and then drops the towel. After staring at her for a few moments, Mark hands over the three hundred dollars.

The wife takes the money, wraps herself in the towel again, and goes back upstairs.

"Who was at the door?" her husband asks.

"It was Mark," she says.

"Oh," says the husband. "Did he say anything about the three hundred dollars he owes me?"

LIFE LESSON

There's a pretty good business lesson here: Keep your eyes open and always be ready to take advantage of a windfall. If you're clever enough—or lucky enough—to recognize an opportunity when it appears in front of you (like the neighbor), you might find a way to squeeze extra value out of any experience.

BEYOND THE PUNCH LINE

Recognizing opportunity starts with an ability to see things from new perspectives. And that takes practice. Here are three ways to nurture that talent:

1. **Seek out creative people.** They're called creative because they can create things—books, poems, films, paintings, music, sculptures, you name it—from scratch. This skill gives them the ability to see something where others see nothing. You can learn a lot about finding opportunity from them.

2. **Write things down.** When something surprises you, make a note of it in a journal. When you come up against a problem, put that in your journal too. Got a new idea that you think is pretty good? Put it in your journal. Recording this information

in writing will help you to keep track of opportunities you'd miss if you just let the information fade from memory.

3. **Embrace new ideas.** If a new idea seems too risky, too expensive, too difficult, or too unrealistic, resist the temptation to dismiss it out of hand. Strip away your negative bias and really mull it over. You may realize that the idea is daring, not deadly, and worth pursuing (see Joke 8).

——— 46 ———

In Confidence

"Education is when you read the fine print.
Experience is what you get if you don't."
—Pete Seeger

Four lawyers—two senior partners and two junior associates—were traveling to a conference by train. At the station, the junior associates watched as the senior partners bought a single ticket.

"How can you both travel on one ticket?" asked one of the younger lawyers.

"Watch and learn," said a senior partner.

They all boarded the train and the junior associates took their seats, but the senior partners squeezed into a restroom and closed the door behind them. Soon after the train left the station, the conductor came around to collect tickets. He knocked on the bathroom door. "Tickets, please," he said. The door opened a crack and one arm appeared, holding a ticket. The conductor took the ticket and moved on.

The junior associates were impressed by this trick. So on the return trip, the senior partners suggested they try it too. But as the junior partners were buying their single ticket, they were surprised to see that the senior partners weren't buying any tickets at all.

"How can you travel without a ticket?" asked one of the young lawyers.

"Watch and learn," said a senior partner.

They all boarded the train, and the junior associates squeezed into one bathroom while the senior partners squeezed into another one nearby. Soon after the train left the station, one of the senior partners emerged and walked over to the bathroom where the junior partners were hiding. He knocked on the bathroom door and said, "Tickets, please."

LIFE LESSON

The lure of getting "something for free" can cloud your judgment . . . and makes you really vulnerable to scam artists.

Don't trust a scammer. Ever. If they're cheating another person, it's a safe bet they'll do it to you too. Don't be fooled into thinking you're on the same side. You're never on the same side as a con man—they're only out for themselves. And remember: A good con artist never seems like a con artist. They seem like someone you can trust—which is what makes them successful. You don't realize you're a victim until you're left without a ticket on a moving train.

BEYOND THE PUNCH LINE

A "con artist" (from "*confidence* artist") specializes in gaining your confidence . . . so they can cheat you. They may be well-dressed, personable, and convincing. And what they offer you may be incredibly attractive. But it's all designed to get your attention and then part you from your money by appealing to two things: your need and your greed.

• **Your emotional need.** Does the thought of making a donation to a worthy nonprofit appeal to you? That's a perfect opening for a con artist. Our brains produce a hormone called oxytocin that makes us feel good when we help other people. So you give them the money and feel good that you've helped. But they keep the money . . . and probably ask you for more.

• **Your financial need.** Are you out of work? Up to your eyeballs in debt? You may not know it, but there's a target on your back. Con artists know that a too-good-to-be-true "opportunity" won't seem like a scam to you—it will sound like a lifeline.

• **Your greed.** Who doesn't want to make a pile of money? Once greed is triggered, anything can happen—we abandon ethics, ignore logic, and fall for lines like "once-in-a-lifetime opportunity" and "you can't lose." If someone's offering a "huge return" on a "hot tip" or a "no-risk" deal, they're appealing to your greed. If the deal is long on promise but short on detail, that's a good indication you're being scammed.

----- 47 -----

Who's Driving?

"The past is never dead. It's not even past."
—**William Faulkner**

During a taxi ride, the passenger taps the cab driver on the shoulder to ask him a question. The driver screams, loses control of the car, nearly hits a bus, drives up onto the sidewalk, and stops just inches away from a shop window. For a second everything goes quiet in the cab. Then the driver says, "Look, buddy, don't ever do that again. You scared the daylights out of me!"

The passenger, completely shaken, says, "Geez, I'm really sorry. I didn't realize that a little tap would scare you so much."

The driver thinks for a minute, and finally replies, "That's okay; it's not really your fault. Today is my first day as a cab driver. For the last twenty-five years, I've been driving a hearse."

LIFE LESSON

Sometimes we think we're reacting to events in the present when we're actually reliving the past—unconsciously responding to the ghosts of old experiences. It can have disastrous results: If you're not aware that past experiences are "driving the bus," then you're not in control and anything can happen.

BEYOND THE PUNCH LINE

Events that bring up memories or reactions from the past are known as *triggers*, because they trigger a reaction that's out of proportion to whatever caused it. We all have them. For example, if a dog bit you when you were a child, you might get anxious whenever a dog approaches—even if it's a small, friendly one. If your parents bossed you around when you were young, you might get irrationally angry whenever someone tells you what to do. And so on.

If you want to find out more about what triggers you, here are some strategies:

• **Ask someone you trust.** It might be obvious to people who know you well. They've been observing you for a long time.

• **Ask yourself whether you're reacting or responding.** Responding is thoughtful and in the moment. Reacting is automatic and emotional.

• **Use your experience.** When you overreact to something, take time to consider what happened and what you could have done differently. With that, map out an alternative scenario and mentally place yourself in it. Psychologists say that if you do this consistently, you'll increase your ability to modify future behavior.

Local Hero

*"Be patient and tough. Someday this pain
will be useful to you."*
—Ovid

D r. Epstein, a world-renowned physician, was invited back to his hometown to give a public lecture. On the evening of the talk, the auditorium was packed with friends, acquaintances, and people who were proud of their native son. He walked onto the dais in the big auditorium and placed his papers on the lectern, but they slid off and hit the floor.

As he bent over to retrieve the papers, he inadvertently farted. And because his rear end was so close to the microphone, the amplified sound reverberated throughout the entire building.

The doctor was mortified, but somehow kept his composure just long enough to deliver his speech. When he was done, he raced out the stage door, vowing never to set foot in his hometown again.

Decades later, he returned to visit his elderly mother, who was very ill. He arrived under cover of darkness and checked into his hotel under the name Levy.

"Is this your first visit to our town, Mr. Levy?" asked the hotel clerk.

"No, young man," replied Dr. Epstein. "I grew up here. I moved away a long time ago, though."

"And you never visit?" asked the clerk.

"Well, actually I did visit once, but I had a very embarrassing experience and I didn't feel I could come back and face the people here."

"Mr. Levy," offered the clerk, "far be it from me to give advice to such a distinguished gentleman as yourself, but one thing I've learned in my young life is that often what seems embarrassing to me isn't even noticed by others. And that's probably the case with your incident too."

"Thank you, but I doubt that's true of my incident," said Dr. Epstein.

"Why? Was it a long time ago?"

"Yes, it was a long time ago."

"Oh," said the clerk. "Was it before or after the Epstein Fart?"

LIFE LESSON

Sometimes things really *are* as bad as they seem. But that doesn't change anything: You still have to keep going and live your life. What makes that possible is a quality called *resilience*: the ability to bounce back when things don't go as planned.

Does that sound impossibly heroic? It's not. Resilience is a normal part of being human, and studies show that you can always develop it.

Being resilient doesn't mean you won't feel pain. There's no way to avoid that. But it does mean that you'll have the strength to get through tough times—and live to fart another day.

BEYOND THE PUNCH LINE

According to multiple studies, the biggest enemy of resilience is "a sense of powerlessness." A series of experiments in the 1970s revealed that when we feel powerless to change our circumstances, we're inclined to just give up and accept them. But the studies also suggested that we can fight back and build resilience. Some tips for how to do that:

1. **Lose the "loser" mentality.** Do you tend to internalize setbacks as "proof" of your incompetence or low self-worth? A lot of us do, but resilient people take failure as a chance to learn and improve.

2. **Goal up.** Working toward specific goals and honoring commitments gives us incentive to bounce back. This applies to business, personal relationships, or even volunteer work. One key: Try to keep the goals manageable. Reaching them empowers you; not reaching them can make you feel like a failure.

3. **Mission: control.** Resilient people have an internal locus of control (see Joke 40); they feel in charge of their own fate, and resist victimization. They maintain this by focusing on things they can control, not on things they can't.

4. **Look on the bright side.** Resilient people know that any setback is just one event—they don't globalize it. They regard difficulties as temporary and they anticipate improvement.

5. **Phone a friend.** Studies show that the number-one factor in developing resilience is having strong family and social connections. Nurturing, primary relationships actually make you a stronger person.

———— 49 ————

Don't Ask

*"God may forgive sins . . . but awkwardness
has no forgiveness in heaven or earth."*
—Ralph Waldo Emerson

A woman walks up to an old man sitting in a rocking chair on his porch. "Excuse me," she says. "You look so happy. If you don't mind my asking, what's your secret for a long and happy life?"

"Well," the man replies, "every day I smoke two packs of cigarettes, drink a pint of whiskey, eat a dozen doughnuts and a bag of potato chips, and I never exercise."

"Wow! That's incredible," she says. "Exactly how old are you?"

"Twenty-six."

LIFE LESSON

Who hasn't asked an embarrassing question based on some-one's appearance? Curious or careless, we forget we're dealing with people's feelings and casually inquire, "When is the baby due?"—and it turns out the woman's not pregnant. Or we ask a person who's struggling financially why they don't "just buy" something they need. At that point we aren't just embarrass-ing ourselves—we're being unintentionally cruel, and it can cause deep emotional pain.

Before you blurt out a personal question, consider its impact. Remind yourself that genuinely connecting with someone starts with showing respect for their feelings. Or just keep it simple: Make it a rule to avoid potentially embarrass-ing questions about potentially sensitive issues altogether. It can save you (and others) a lot of distress.

BEYOND THE PUNCH LINE

Here's a list of ten sensitive questions you probably shouldn't ask. Just consider how you'd feel if someone asked them of you.

1. "Are you pregnant?"

2. "How much money do you make?"

3. "When are you having kids?"

4. "How much do you weigh?" (Or worse: "Have you gained weight?")

5. "What are you?"

6. "Is something wrong with your health?"

7. "Are you two planning to get married?"

8. "Why can't you afford that?"

9. "Still single?"

10. "What's that?" (pointing to scar or body marker)

If you do put your foot in your mouth with one of these questions, here are two ways to deal with it:

1. A sincere apology. The good news is that because practically everyone's done this at some time, the person will probably understand. And sincerity is a great balm for almost everything.

2. If that's not possible, try using a third party—someone you both trust—to approach them with your message. Again, the person is likely to appreciate that you're making the effort. Ask your mutual friend to offer your contact info so you can smooth things over.

—— 50 ——

MYOB
(Mind Your Own Business)

"Let every fox take care of its own tail."
—Italian proverb

A little guy is sitting at a bar, just staring at his drink, when a big biker walks up to him, takes the drink, and gulps it down.

The little guy starts crying. The biker says, "Hey, man. I was just joking. Here, I'll buy you another drink."

"No, it's not that. This is the worst day of my life. First, I overslept and missed an important meeting, so my boss fired me. Then, when I left the building, I discovered that my car had been stolen and the police said there was nothing they could do about it. So I took a cab home, but accidentally left my wallet in there, and the cab driver just drove away. Then I found my wife in bed with my best friend. So I walked out and came to this bar. And just when I was thinking about putting an end to my life, you show up and drink my poison."

LIFE LESSON

Butting into someone else's life can have disastrous results. Interfering with their problems is *like* drinking their poison—and you already know how that will work out. The antidote: Fight the impulse and learn to mind your own business.

BEYOND THE PUNCH LINE

Here are a few tips:

1. Be clear about your role. If it's not really your problem, and no one's asked you to help, MYOB. Can't tell if it affects you? Try this simple trick:

• Write down the problem: for example, "Gordon hates his job." Now draw a circle around it.

• Draw a bigger circle around the problem. Inside that circle, write down the name of the person(s) most directly affected by the issue: for example: "His wife."

• Keep making the circles, adding one person each time (kids, co-workers, boss, etc.) until you see where you fit in. That should clarify it.

2. If no one's invited you into the conversation, they don't want you involved. It doesn't matter if you have an opinion about the topic. MYOB.

3. If you butt in anyway, and they cross their arms while you're talking, don't look you in the eye, or seem to be moving away from you, they don't want your help. MYOB.

—— 51 ——

Getting a Leg Up

"The best way to have a good idea is to have a lot of ideas."
—Linus Pauling

A biologist was experimenting with a big bullfrog. "I want you to jump as far as you can," he said ... and the bullfrog jumped. The biologist took a measurement and wrote in his notebook: "Healthy frog can jump thirty-six inches." Then he cut off the frog's right front leg, sealed the wound, and said, "Jump!" Predictably, the jump was a little shorter. The biologist wrote in his notebook: "Removed one leg. Frog can still jump thirty-three inches." Then he cut off the frog's left rear leg. Again he told the frog to jump. After measuring the length of the jump, the biologist wrote: "Removed two legs. Frog can still jump twenty-two inches." The biologist then cut off the frog's left front leg and once again said, "Jump!" The one-legged frog could barely jump at all, and the biologist wrote: "Removed three legs. Frog can jump six inches." Finally, the biologist removed the poor frog's right rear leg and said, "Okay frog, last time. Jump!" He put the frog down and it just sat there motionless. "Jump!" he yelled. Still the bullfrog did nothing. The biologist wrote in his notebook: "Removed fourth leg. Frog has gone deaf."

LIFE LESSON

Scientists frequently come up with bad guesses and ridiculous conclusions—like the biologist in this joke. But scientists don't let that bother them, because they understand that until it's proven, an idea is just an idea. The *scientific method* (see below) allows them to postulate any bizarre notion they want—but then it *requires* them to test their hypothesis to see if it's true. That's why we can be sure that eventually, someone would have tested the biologist's theory and proven it was both nutty *and* wrong.

This approach isn't just for scientists—we all need to understand how to distinguish science fact from science fiction. Otherwise, people can (and will) pass off their crackpot theories as truth—which isn't a good thing for you or society. So be critical of untested "facts," and arm yourself with the simple question "What's the proof?"

BEYOND THE PUNCH LINE

The standard for proving *anything* is the "scientific method." If you paid attention in science class you probably recall this simple set of steps that scientists, inventors, chefs—and pretty much everyone else—use to establish what's true about the physical world. Here's a simplified version:

1. Identify the problem. What do you want to know?

2. Learn as much as you can about the subject.

3. Come up with a hypothesis. Make an educated guess about what you'll discover.

4. Create an experiment that will tell you whether your hypothesis is true. (Or just as likely, not true.)

5. Analyze the data from the experiment.

6. Come up with a conclusion.

Sounds simple? It is. We often do this naturally, without thinking of it as a formal method, but it's actually one of humanity's greatest achievements. It wasn't until the 1600s that scientists (then called natural philosophers) accepted the idea that we could learn about the world by observation and experimentation. The results are all around you: cars, computers, medicines, you name it. The modern world couldn't exist without the scientific method—because it works.

52

Get in Line

"A man that studieth revenge, keeps his own wounds green, which otherwise would heal."
—**Francis Bacon**

Ayoung woman is walking home one day when she spots an odd funeral procession on its way to the cemetery. A black hearse is being followed by a second hearse. Behind that is an older woman walking with a pit bull on a leash, followed by a hundred women walking single file behind her.

The young woman watches for a few minutes in wonder, and finally approaches the woman walking the dog.

"Excuse me," she says, "I'm sorry to bother you in your time of grief, but I've never seen anything like this. Whose funeral is it?"

"My husband's," the older woman answers. "He's in the first hearse. This dog found him in bed with his girlfriend and killed both of them. She's in the second hearse."

The young woman says, "Oh, I'm sorry" . . . but then smiles and adds, "Say, can I borrow your dog?"

"Get in line," the woman answers.

LIFE LESSON

Revenge is one of our most basic human instincts. We believe that inflicting pain on people who've "wronged" us will make us feel better. But it doesn't really work that way: In studies, most people who pursue revenge report feeling worse, not better—their anger actually increases. Looking for revenge, it turns out, keeps us immersed in toxic feelings. That may be what Confucius meant when he said, "If you seek revenge, first dig two graves."

So when you feel like getting even, ask yourself whether revenge is a commitment you really want to make. It's not only a commitment to making someone else feel bad; it's probably a commitment to feeling bad yourself, and to being stuck in the past. When you're focused on revenge, you don't get to move on with your life—you just get to relive some of its most unpleasant moments.

BEYOND THE PUNCH LINE

Researchers believe that humans are hardwired to seek revenge as a way to enforce social cooperation. They've found that we experience revenge (or at least thoughts about it) in the reward center of the brain—so it's literally a pleasure to ponder. But it doesn't work as promised. Experts recommend taking these steps to avoid getting sucked into seeking revenge:

1. **Accept it.** The desire for revenge feels like a call to action, but, in fact, there's no correlation between feeling it and needing to do something about it. You feel it because you're human. No response is required. Let the feeling pass if you can.

2. **Pause.** Give yourself time to process the experience. Refrain from making any decisions until you've calmed down and can think intelligently. Studies suggest that choosing not to act is a way of communicating to yourself that the matter is trivial, which makes it easier to let go.

3. **Figure out what you really need.** The desire for revenge comes from a feeling of being violated. What you may need in this situation is vindication, not retaliation—restoring self-respect and getting acknowledgment that you've been wronged. There are other ways to restore self-respect besides fighting back. For example, put the "revenge energy" into working toward personal goals, keeping the focus on your-self—not on your "adversary."

53

Pushing Buttons

*"The last of the human freedoms [is] to choose one's attitude
in any given set of circumstances . . ."*
—Viktor Frankl

An old man and a young man were playing a
friendly round of golf. On the eighth hole, both
men sliced their tee shots and ended up in the
rough, where a hundred-foot pine tree stood between
them and the green. It looked like they'd need an extra
stroke just to get the ball back onto the fairway. "I guess
neither of us will be getting a birdie this hole," said the
young man.

"Why do you say that?" asked the older man.

"We're too close to that tree. There's no way we can
get the ball over it."

"Seriously?" said the older man. "I'm surprised you're
such a wimp. Why, when I was your age, I hit the ball clear
over that tree with ease."

"What? Well, if you did it then," replied the younger
man angrily, "I can do it now."

"Really? Want to bet?" asked the old man.

"Sure. Fifty bucks says I can hit it over the pine tree."

The old man nodded in agreement as the young man squared up over the ball, looked up at the tree, and brought his backswing as far back as he could. Then he launched the ball higher than he'd ever hit a ball. And it went directly into the middle of the tree and got stuck in the branches.

"Of course," the old man grinned, "when I was your age, that tree was only about fifteen feet tall."

LIFE LESSON

At some point, people are going to figure out how to push your buttons—often (like the old guy in the joke) for their own amusement. Somehow, they'll know just what to do to make you feel insecure, angry, or ashamed. You can't prevent that. But you can learn how to use restraint and self-knowledge to keep yourself from being goaded into reacting irrationally, and as a result, gain the confidence that comes with knowing you're capable of being in control when you need to be.

BEYOND THE PUNCH LINE

1. **Find a way to disengage.** Chances are, getting your buttons pushed will come as a surprise. When you suddenly realize what's going on, don't react to it. Calmly go somewhere by yourself and reset your buttons. You'll get control again quicker than you think—and then no one will even know that your buttons were pushed.

2. **Own your buttons.** No one can *make* you feel anything—they can only trigger feelings you already have. So acknowledge that your buttons are about you and no one else. They

represent low self-esteem, shame, insecurity, and a host of other sensitive issues. Once you recognize that, you can come up with a strategy to deal with it. Conversely, by the way, the button-pusher's nastiness is not your problem. Have compassion, but let them find some other way to deal with their own pain.

3. **Set clear boundaries.** Let people know how far they can go before you'll step away—and then stick to it. Examples might include: saying no when you mean no, and not feeling guilty about it; speaking up when you feel mistreated; and not going along just to be a good sport (see Joke 65).

— 54 —

Lost Keys

"Not knowing when the dawn will come,
I open every door"
—**Emily Dickinson**

Q: When you lose your keys, where is the one place you'll always find them?

A: The last place you look.

LIFE LESSON

This classic riddle may be about losing your keys, but to us it's a metaphor for seeking pretty much anything in life. When you're looking for something, there are often moments of anxiety or panic when you're overwhelmed by the feeling of not knowing. It can feel like *you're* the one who's lost, and that you'll never find what you're searching for. But remember: Discovery is just the end point of the process—as soon as you find what you're looking for, you're done. What's important is the search itself. And "not knowing" is an integral part of it.

Try not to confuse looking for something with not being able to find it. You just haven't found it *yet*.

BEYOND THE PUNCH LINE

Why is "not knowing" so difficult? Research indicates that we may be hardwired to feel uncomfortable with uncertainty. In a 2006 study, for example, people "given the choice between waiting for a lesser amount of pain and instantly receiving a greater amount of pain" actually chose *more pain* over the discomfort of waiting. And a 2010 study discovered that our brains "feel rewarded when we make a choice—any choice." So remember that while we're searching we're also struggling against the natural impulse to make quick and easy choices—even if we know they aren't good for us.

Is That Your Final Answer?

"Take calculated risks.
That is quite different from being rash."
—George Patton

Aguy dies and goes to Hell. Satan meets him and explains that he's going to show the man three rooms. "You must choose which room you will spend eternity in," Satan says.

In the first room, people are standing up to their necks in s**t. The guy is horrified and says, "No way, let me see the next room."

In the second room, people are standing up to their noses in s**t. Again, the guy is horrified and says no.

So Satan opens the door to the third room, where people are standing up to their knees in s**t, drinking coffee and eating doughnuts. The guy immediately says, "I'll take this one."

Satan nods and starts to leave as the guy wades into the room and pours himself a cup of coffee. That's when Satan turns and yells, "OK. Coffee break's over. Everyone back on your heads!"

LIFE LESSON

Need to make a quick decision? Try to slow it down and get as much information as you can *before* you make a commitment. Snap judgments can have dire consequences, and some decisions, once you've made them, can commit you to an eternity of . . . well, you know.

BEYOND THE PUNCH LINE

According to behavioral scientists, we can't help making snap judgments. It's a "skill" we develop as infants and use for our entire lives. In a matter of seconds (or, according to some studies, as little as a tenth of a second) we decide if we like or trust someone, whether someone's telling the truth, if a new boss or a potential employee will work out, whether a first date will be pleasant, and so on. Sometimes snap judgments are correct; sometimes they're false. You can improve the odds of making good ones if you're aware that mistakes are commonly made by basing decisions on:

1. **Personal prejudices.** Quick choices can be easily influenced by a personal bias that's not connected to the decision. For instance: a favorite (or least favorite) color, an odor, a disability, etc.

2. **Conventional wisdom.** Our choices are often unduly influenced by social norms. For example: Malcolm Gladwell, author of *Blink*, surveyed several hundred Fortune 500 companies about how tall their CEOs were, and found that they were all tall. "There is no correlation between height and the ability to motivate and lead people," says Gladwell. "But for some reason corporations choose tall people for leadership roles."

We also make quick (but irrational) decisions based on factors like politeness, physical attractiveness, ethnic or gender stereotypes, and so on.

3. **Cultural cues.** Studies have found that we're better at reading the faces of members of our own cultural or racial groups. When you're aware of this, you may have an extra advantage if you find you have to make a quick judgment about someone from a different ethnic group.

——— 56 ———

Love, Actually

"Can the leopard change his spots?"
—**Steve Javna, paraphrasing the Bible (Jeremiah 13:23)**

A bride and groom were blissfully in love and couldn't wait to begin their life together. She loved to ride horses, so they went to a Montana dude ranch for their honeymoon. One day, they decided to go out for a ride. As the horses crossed a small stream, the man's horse slipped and jostled him. When they reached the stream bank, the woman dismounted, walked over to his horse, and staring into its eyes, said, "That's one!" Then she remounted and they continued their ride.

A little farther along the path, the husband's horse stumbled while stepping over a fallen tree. The woman got down and, pointing her finger in the horse's face said, "That's two!" She returned to her saddle and they moved on.

Later that afternoon, the man's horse got spooked by a snake in the path and reared back on its hind legs, throwing the man onto the ground. The woman quickly dismounted, stepped in front of her husband's horse, and shouted, "That's three!" Then she pulled a pistol out of her pocket and shot the horse dead.

The man, shocked at seeing the horse killed, said to his wife, "You maniac! How could you do such a thing?"

The woman walked over to her husband, and, staring calmly into his eyes, said, "That's one."

LIFE LESSON

A person's core values and personality reveal themselves in everything they do. But we often ignore the message because we want them to be somebody else—someone nicer, someone stronger, someone less demanding, someone more loving. Fortunately (or unfortunately) that delusion can only last for so long, because as our father used to tell us, "You can't be two people." Eventually the real person always comes through—and as Maya Angelou famously said, "When someone shows you who they are, believe them."

BEYOND THE PUNCH LINE

Here are five ways people show you who they really are:

1. **Their interaction with strangers.** How do they treat people when there are no immediate social repercussions? For

example, are they polite to waitresses and taxi drivers, or are they rude and dismissive? This says a lot about their level of empathy.

2. **The friends they choose.** Our sense of what's "normal" and socially acceptable is greatly influenced by our friends. Friends also tend to mirror each other's behavior, so observing someone's friends is like viewing a slice of their personality.

3. **How they react when they don't get what they want.** A person's strategy for dealing with the frustration of minor setbacks is a good indicator of how they deal with life in general. The more flexible they are, the better they are at rolling with life's punches. Getting angry when small goals are thwarted is considered a sign of low self-esteem and poor adaptive ability.

4. **Keeping (or not keeping) commitments.** There are many reasons why a person may not keep commitments. They may agree to do something just because they're confrontation averse. They might have a narcissist's callous disregard for other people. Or they might mean well but be unrealistic about time. The bottom line is still the same in all cases: If they don't keep their promises to others, don't expect them to keep promises to you.

5. **How they've resolved past relationships.** Do they get along with previous partners, friends, and family members? Have they learned from failed relationships? Imagine yourself among that group. That can help you see them more clearly.

57

Bad News

"Bad news isn't wine. It doesn't improve with age."
—Colin Powell

A woman goes on vacation and leaves her cat with her sister. A few days later she calls and asks her sister how the cat is doing.

"Bad news," says the sister. "Your cat died."

The woman gets furious. "That's how you tell me my beloved cat is gone? You should have said something like, 'The cat's on the roof and we can't get it down.' And then when I called the next day you could have said, 'The cat came down off the roof, but it's in really bad shape and the vet doesn't think the poor thing is going to make it.' And when I called the next day, *then* you could have told me the cat died!"

"I'm really sorry," said the sister.

"I'm sorry too," the woman said after a long pause. "I guess I shouldn't have snapped at you like that. You know, it was just such a shock. Anyway, how's Mom?"

"Umm . . . she's on the roof and we can't get her down."

LIFE LESSON

OK, so what *is* a good way to deliver bad news? Answer: There is none. It's called "bad news" for a reason—it's bad.

Bad news is almost always painful, which is why most of us try to avoid it. But it's also part of life, so we really can't. However, if you learn how to deliver bad news in a way that works for you *and* for the person on the receiving end, you're more likely to tackle it in a timely way—which is smart, because the news doesn't get any better if you put it off. And here's the good news about delivering bad news: Once you've put it behind you, it's a relief.

BEYOND THE PUNCH LINE

Here are some tips to help make delivering bad news less bad:

1. **Do it in person.** It's a way to show respect. Plus, you can respond to questions or clarify the situation—which means you're less likely to be misunderstood.

2. **Do it as soon as possible.** Again, it shows respect . . . but it also prevents the bad news from festering in *you*. If it requires action, delays can compound the problem. As Napoléon said: "Never awake me when you have good news to announce, because with good news nothing presses; but when you have bad news, arouse me immediately, for then there is not an instant to be lost."

3. **Use the "sandwich" method.** Start with something positive, give the bad news, then end with something positive. This doesn't work if it's fake. Be genuine.

4. **Show empathy.** If it's appropriate, offer comfort (see Joke 22).

5. **Don't make it a surprise.** Find a way to telegraph that you're delivering bad news before getting into it. Give the recipient (and yourself) a moment to prepare for it emotionally.

6. **Tell the truth.** Well, maybe not all of it. But don't withhold facts that might help the person understand the situation better.

7. **Pay attention to where you are.** Is it private? Is there a place to sit? Is there too much noise? Can the person exit easily if they want to? These things matter, so choose the location carefully.

8. **Let them react.** You can't deliver bad news and expect the other person to remain calm. But however they react, *you* should remain calm. You can't change the news, but you can make it feel better . . . or worse.

58

Take the Money and Run?

"All things come to him who waits—
provided he knows what he is waiting for."
—Woodrow Wilson

A barber is talking to one of his customers. "See that kid?" he says as he points to a twelve-year-old standing outside the barbershop. "He is the dumbest kid in the world. Watch. I'll prove it to you." The barber takes out a one-dollar bill and a five-dollar bill, and then calls the boy inside. He holds out both bills, and asks, "Which one do you want, son?"

The kid takes the one-dollar bill and leaves the shop.

"See?" laughs the barber. "The dumbest kid in the world."

A few minutes after the customer leaves the barbershop, he happens to see the boy coming out of an ice cream store. He goes over and asks, "If you don't mind my asking, son, why didn't you take the five-dollar bill?"

The boy takes a lick of his ice cream cone and replies, "Because the day I choose the five-dollar bill, the game's over."

LIFE LESSON

It's a lifelong dilemma: Should you go for instant gratification or long-term satisfaction? Should we order the bacon cheese-burger or the salad? Go out with friends or stay home and study?

But there's more to consider here than just what to eat or whether to go out partying. It turns out there are measurable benefits to learning to wait, and cultivating delayed gratification is really an opportunity to develop a life skill that can impact your entire existence. That doesn't mean you should *never* go for immediate gratification. But if you want to get more out of life, at some point you need to learn how to be focused and disciplined—rather than just grabbing the five-dollar bill.

BEYOND THE PUNCH LINE

A lot of what we know about the benefits of delayed gratification comes from the famous Stanford marshmallow experiment. In 1960, Stanford University professor Walter Mischel created a test in which he brought a group of four- to six-year-olds into a room, one at a time, and put a sweet treat—a marshmallow, a cookie, or a brownie—on a table in front of them. Each child was told that they could eat the treat, or wait fifteen minutes and get two treats. Then he left the room and watched on a monitor to see what the children did. Not surprisingly, plenty of kids ate the treat as soon as he left the room. Others tried to wait... and failed. But about a third of the kids managed to wait the entire fifteen minutes without eating the marshmallow.

For the next fifty years, the Stanford research team tracked the children to see if there was any correlation between the ability to delay gratification and success later in life. The answer was surprising even to them: They found that the children who'd been able to delay gratification were more reliable, more proactive, did better in school, found better jobs, and earned higher salaries. They also were better able to concentrate and manage stress, and were less prone to obesity, alcoholism, and drug addiction. The last study, in 2011, showed that these characteristics remained with the individuals for life.

Research since then indicates that the ability to delay gratification isn't innate, as researchers originally believed—it can be learned. Here are three suggestions:

1. Dr. Mischel believes the key is to replace the compelling "instant gratification" image with a less appealing one. For example, replace a mental image of French fries with a plate of carrots, or someone having a heart attack from eating too many fries. Or just imagine that the restaurant is out of fries.

2. Cultivate an ability to imagine the future and how your actions will affect it. A study at Washington University showed that the brains of people who delay gratification light up in the *anterior prefrontal cortex*, the area that helps us think about the future.

3. Researchers at the University of Rochester found that kids living in an environment where they receive what they are promised are more willing to wait for a reward in the future. You can build up that trust with yourself: Set small tasks that are easy to achieve, promise yourself small rewards when you achieve them, and keep the promise. Be consistent about it, because that's the secret to building trust. And when you've learned to trust the promise, you'll be better able to delay gratification.

59

You're Bad Luck

"Don't believe everything you think."
—folk wisdom

As a man lay on his deathbed, he motioned for his wife to come closer. "My darling," he said, "you've been right there beside me through everything life's thrown at me." His wife reached down and tenderly held his hand. The man continued, "When I lost my job, you were there. And when the house burned down... when my business went bankrupt... when I had my heart attack—you were right there beside me." He looked up at her. "And now that I'm nearing the end of the road, I've finally come to a realization."

"What's that, dear?" she asked sweetly.

"You're bad luck."

LIFE LESSON

Sometimes we add two and two and come up with five. That's why it's good to remember this phrase: *Correlation does not imply causation.* It means that even though two things occur simultaneously, we shouldn't assume one is causing the other. In fact, they might not be related at all. This may sound obvious, but as the joke illustrates, people often link events in head-scratching ways. For instance, if your favorite team won while you were wearing your lucky green shirt, was your shirt a factor? (Some people would actually say yes.)

Human brains are built to look for patterns in our environment, especially for events that seem to demonstrate cause and effect. After all, our survival as a species depended on being able to figure out that eating a certain kind of plant will kill us, or that sticking your hand into a fire will burn it. Most of the time we get this right, but sometimes we see patterns where they don't really exist. So we need to be wary of our own and others' faulty reasoning—even if it appears to be perfectly logical. Believing in a lucky shirt won't hurt you, but when you base decisions about relationships, health, or business on irrational logic, the outcome can be devastating.

BEYOND THE PUNCH LINE

Here are three common factors that people misinterpret as causation:

1. Coincidence.

Example: You notice that whenever there's a full moon, a particular stock goes up. So you time your investment to coincide with the next full moon . . . and the stock tumbles. The correlation was just coincidence.

Real-life example: Each year from 1999 to 2009, whenever Nicholas Cage made more movies, the number of Americans who fell into swimming pools and drowned increased. When he made fewer movies, the number decreased. Were Cage's films responsible for the drowning deaths? Of course not—the correlation was a coincidence.

2. A confounding variable.

Example: You note that whenever you wear shorts, your spouse seems happier. So you wear them all the time . . . but it doesn't seem to change anything. Why? Because at first you were only wearing shorts in warm weather, and it was the warm weather—not the shorts—that elevated your spouse's mood. Warm weather was the confounding variable.

Real-life examples:

• People who fall asleep with their shoes on are more likely to wake up with a headache. Why? Drunken people are more likely to fall asleep without undressing . . . and wake up with a hangover. The confounding variable is inebriation.

• People with bigger feet are more likely to be literate. Why? People with bigger feet are more likely to be adults, and adults are more literate than children. The confounding variable is age.

3. Reverse causation.

Example: You notice that whenever windmills spin faster, there's more wind. So you assume that the windmills are causing the wind. Obviously you have that backward.

Real-life example: Someone at serious risk for heart disease changes to a healthier diet and dies of a heart attack. Statistically, it might appear that they died of a heart attack because they switched to a healthier diet, and you might reject changing your diet because, after all, it might kill you.

60

Don't Get Bugged

"There are no rules here.
We're trying to accomplish something."
—Thomas Edison

O ne evening over dinner, a boy asked his father, "Dad, are bugs good to eat?"

"That's disgusting," the father replied. "You know the rules—we don't talk about things like that while we're eating."

After dinner the dad asked, "Now, what was it you wanted, son?"

"Oh, never mind, Dad," the boy said. "There was a bug in your soup, but now it's gone."

LIFE LESSON

Sure, we all know rules are essential. But if you stick to them too inflexibly, sooner or later you'll wind up "eating bugs." And you'll probably deserve it.

BEYOND THE PUNCH LINE

Here are four times when it's a good idea to bend (or even break) a rule:

• **If no one really understands it.** People keep asking you to clarify it and you can't.

• **If it's so old, no one knows why it's there in the first place.** "That's the way we've always done it" is not a reason—it's a habit.

• **If it's pissing people off.** We expect rules to be fair. If people are complaining, chances are your rule is not.

• **If it's the right thing to do.** Sometimes making life better for another human being is all that matters.

—— 61 ——

Water Torture

"Dripping water hollows out stone,
not through force but through persistence."
—Ovid

An astrophysicist is giving a lecture at a local university about the fate of the solar system. "The sun is now in the middle of its life cycle," he explains to the audience. "In about five billion years it will become a red giant and shortly after, it will explode."

Suddenly a woman in the back of the lecture hall jumps up and shouts, "*How* many years did you say?"

"About five billion," the scientist answers.

"Oh, thank God," the woman replies, visibly relieved. "I thought you said five *million*."

LIFE LESSON

How often do *you* find yourself excited or upset about things that have no real impact on your life? Are you secretly thrilled by a celebrity romance? Are you outraged by the latest scandal in the news? Everyone is susceptible to that kind of distraction. Politicians understand this and use it to lure us into voting for them. Advertisers use it to sell us products we don't need. News organizations capitalize on it every day. But you don't have to take their bait. When you find yourself engrossed by something that on reflection turns out to be irrelevant—let it go. It's an enormous relief to get rid of that extra baggage . . . and really, haven't we all got more important things to think about?

BEYOND THE PUNCH LINE

You may think of celebrity gossip and petty political scandals as inconsequential background noise. But they're actually quite corrosive. Contrary to what you might expect, research has shown that the human brain deals better with major crises than with small, persistent annoyances. Why? Think about the difference between a broken water pipe and a dripping faucet. If it's a big leak, we're programmed to go into emergency mode, call the plumber, and get it fixed. A small leak, on the other hand, is less urgent (we might not even notice it) and may be left unrepaired . . . so it can do a lot of damage over time.

Things like gossip and petty scandal may feel to us like broken water pipes, but they're actually dripping faucets. There's no way to resolve or get rid of them. After all, you can't fix a Hollywood marriage. And you can't stop politicians from lying. So once you start worrying about them, they stay in your system—unless you make a conscious effort to root them out.

If you're trying to determine whether something really matters, ask yourself: Will I care about it a year from now? Will I even remember it a year from now? How about in ten years? If the answer is no, you can let out a sigh of relief and admit that whatever you're worried about probably isn't that important after all.

— 62 —

Old Faithful

"If you would know the road ahead,
ask someone who has traveled it."
—Chinese proverb

Two young salmon are swimming along one day, when they're passed by an older, wiser fish headed the other way.

The old fish greets them as he passes, saying, "Morning boys, how's the water?"

The two young fish continue to swim in silence for a while. Finally, the first one turns to the other and asks, "What the hell is water?"

LIFE LESSON

Knowledge really does come with age and experience. It may not seem that way, but when you're young, your awareness of how the world works—or even what's happening right around you—is limited. So if you want to expand your perspective, try talking to an older, more experienced person about things that are important to you. You might find they actually know something useful.

BEYOND THE PUNCH LINE

For most of human history, societies were illiterate. There was no way to store accumulated knowledge, so the elders of the community served as living libraries and were regularly sought out for advice about life's problems. A lot has changed since then, but one thing that hasn't is that older people are still a prime source of knowledge. You will benefit from their advice, and they will feel valued when you seek them out.

Cornell gerontologist Karl Pillemer's Legacy Project has been collecting "practical advice for living" from America's elders since 2004. Pillemer and his research staff recommend using questions like these to begin a conversation with elders:

1. What would you tell a young person if they asked you to name the most important things you've learned in your life?

2. I've heard that valuable lessons often come from difficult experiences. Did that happen to you? What are some examples?

3. I wonder if there were any big turning points in your life. Was there something that seemed to change everything for you?

4. What have you learned about being happy and successful that you didn't know when you were younger?

5. What do you think I should do now to avoid having regrets when I get older?

63

Expect the Unexpected

*"If I always appear prepared, it is because before
entering an undertaking, I have meditated long and
have foreseen what might occur. It is not genius that
reveals to me suddenly and secretly what I should
do in circumstances unexpected by others; it is
thought and preparation."*
—Napoléon Bonaparte

After thirty years of marriage, a couple was celebrating their sixtieth birthdays together. Knowing she loved antiques, the husband gave his wife a beautiful brass oil lamp as a gift. When she unwrapped it, a genie suddenly appeared. To thank them for freeing him from the lamp, he granted them each one wish. The wife went first and because they'd never had a chance to travel, asked for trip around the world. The genie waved his hand in the air and *poof!* she found herself holding two first-class tickets for an all-expenses-paid world cruise. Then it was the husband's turn. After thinking for a moment, he said, "I wish my wife was thirty years younger than me." The genie waved his hand in the air and *poof!* he was ninety.

LIFE LESSON

This guy clearly didn't think things through before he made his wish. Result: He was nailed by the law of unintended consequences. Actually, there's no way to inoculate yourself against the effects of this law—every decision in life produces at least *some* unexpected results. In the best-case scenario, you get what you want, plus some unplanned benefits; and in the worst-case scenario . . . well, that's the joke.

So think carefully before you act and stay conscious of the fact that there's always more than one possible result to any action you take. Even when you think you have it figured out, there may be a wrinkle you haven't considered. If you plunge ahead without that awareness, you're courting disaster.

BEYOND THE PUNCH LINE

The law of unintended consequences is a real thing—the concept was introduced by sociologist Robert Merton in 1936. Merton speculated that five factors cause it: "Ignorance, misinterpreting the problem, short-term thinking when long-term thinking is called for, values that prohibit taking action, and a self-defeating prophesy." (Merton came up with that term too—see Joke 92.) While there's no way to prevent unintended consequences, there are things you can do to minimize the chance of "perverse results."

Here are four suggestions:

1. **Always analyze your decision from both sides.** Look at potential benefits *and* potential problems, but do it over a period of time. Give yourself time to get over the initial excitement, when you're still seduced by the idea of benefits. Let the ideas percolate and they'll become clearer.

2. Try to avoid impulsive decisions. If a quick decision seems called for, see Joke 55.

3. Get additional perspectives. Often other people can plainly see what's invisible to you. Keep your question simple and direct, like: "What can go wrong here?" or "What problems am I missing?"

4. Do some research. Don't neglect this. The Internet makes research easy, and it can provide critical information about other people's experiences—which can give you insight into possible unexpected outcomes.

64

Kind of a Drag

"In polite society, we call our obsessions hobbies."
—Stephen King

Awoman is starting to get worried because her husband hasn't come back from his regular Saturday afternoon golf game. He's not answering his cell phone, and as the hours pass she gets more and more frantic until finally, at 8:00 p.m., the husband pulls into the driveway.

"Where have you been?" his wife asks angrily. "You should've been home hours ago."

"I'm really sorry, honey," he says. "But I couldn't help it. Harry had a heart attack on the third hole."

"Oh, my God! That's terrible," the wife cries.

"You're telling *me*," he answers. "All day long it was, hit the ball, drag Harry, hit the ball, drag Harry . . ."

LIFE LESSON
Researchers have found that hobbies are beneficial for our emotional and physical health. They reduce negative stress and increase *eustress*, "the positive kind of stress people need to remain feeling excited about life." Hobbies help lower blood pressure and fight depression. They can even help with weight control.

But when passion devolves into obsession, hobbies can become destructive. They can make us blind to almost any antisocial behavior and can wreak havoc on relationships, work, and even bank accounts. Keep an eye out: If any of this starts to sound familiar, you may want to make a few changes—before your behavior becomes a punch line.

BEYOND THE PUNCH LINE

Five ways experts suggest you can keep a hobby from becoming an obsession:

1. **Break up your routine.** Addictions can flourish whenever you get too used to any situation or condition. The problem: It becomes too uncomfortable to make a change, so you just keep doing what you're doing—even if you don't really want to. To avoid this trap, take an intentional break every now and then.

2. **Set a budget.** Figure out how much you can afford to spend on your hobby every month and don't spend one penny more on it. It's a good indication that a hobby has turned into an obsession when the hobbyist won't set limits and doesn't stick to a budget.

3. **Set time limits.** This is a simple way of keeping your hobby a hobby. Decide on a reasonable amount of time to spend on it, and if you stick to the time limit, your hobby will never turn into a habit.

4. **Switch hobbies every once in a while.** If you're a knitter, put down the knitting needles and go bike riding instead. If you make model airplanes, try alternating that with another hobby, like playing tennis. Changing up your hobbies will help

prevent you from becoming too obsessive about any single activity.

5. **Share your hobby with friends and family.** Do you view social obligations as "distractions" from your hobby? Involving friends and family is a good way of maintaining those important relationships and keeping your hobby in perspective.

—— 65 ——

Don't Just Do It

"I am thankful for all the difficult people in my life.
They have shown me exactly who I do not want to be."
—seen on a coffee mug

A group of first-year medical students was in an anatomy class—their first with a real, dead human body. They all gathered around the dissection table as the professor stood by the cadaver—which was covered with a white sheet—and lectured them. "In the practice of medicine, you must have two important qualities. The first is this: Never be disgusted by anything involving the human body."

To make his point, the professor drew back the sheet, stuck a finger in the corpse's butt, pulled it out, and then sucked his finger. "Now you do it," he told them. Stunned, the students hesitated at first. But eventually each one walked up to the body, stuck a finger in the butt, and sucked on it.

When everyone was done, the professor looked at them and said, "The second important quality you need is to be observant. I stuck in my middle finger and sucked on my index finger. Now, learn to pay attention."

LIFE LESSON

You probably think the lesson here is "pay attention" or "be observant." Both are important, so if that's what you take from this joke, fine. But there's another lesson: Don't blindly follow someone who encourages you to do something you know is wrong or dangerous. Say no, even if the person is an authority. Everyone in that class must have suspected the teacher's demonstration was nuts. But they participated anyway. Of course it's only a joke, but think about it—the professor could have stopped the first person before they touched the cadaver and would still have been able to make the same point. But he didn't, and that's abusive.

BEYOND THE PUNCH LINE

According to a 2012 study, about 17 million American workers have abusive supervisors. These abusive relationships aren't just annoying. They threaten people's health by adding unrelenting stress—which is linked to numerous ailments, from heart disease to ulcers.

So what do you do when you're caught in an abusive situation? The simplest thing is to just leave and move on. But if you can't (or don't want to), experts suggest these possible alternatives:

• **Stay civil and courteous, and don't respond.** Don't engage on the abuser's level. Fighting fire with fire doesn't work—it just ignites a bigger fire. But it turns out that being nice doesn't work either. Researchers in a 2015 workplace study were surprised to find that abusive supervisors "did not respond to [their employees] being positive, compassionate, supportive, or helpful." So just wait patiently until they're over it.

• **Stand your ground.** Some people will only feel better if they've done something to actively stick up for themselves. But because fighting back will probably make the situation worse, the trick is to resist surreptitiously. Example: Pretend you don't understand what the boss is talking about . . . or listen, but then do something different.

• **Set boundaries.** Don't take the attacks personally. Take care of yourself, even if it means just walking away. "If they are losing it," says the lead author of the study on abusive bosses, "give them twenty minutes and then they're over it. If you take it personally, you'll fuel it further and they'll continue arguing because it's easy."

66

Scared Straight

"Nothing in life is to be feared. It is only to be understood."
—Marie Curie

Aman receives a parrot as a gift. The bird has a bad attitude; every word out of its mouth is laced with profanity. The man tries to improve the parrot's attitude by using polite language, playing classical music, and anything else he can think of, but nothing changes the bird's vocabulary. Finally, one day the man can't take it anymore; in a fit of temper, he throws the cursing bird into the freezer.

The parrot squawks and screams for a few minutes, but then, suddenly . . . there's total quiet. Afraid that he may have harmed the bird, the man quickly opens the freezer door. The parrot calmly steps out and says, "Sir, I fear I may have offended you with my inappropriate language and rude behavior. Please accept my sincere apology. I assure you that in the future I shall act in a manner more in keeping with your expectations."

The man is stunned by the abrupt change in the parrot's attitude. But before he can ask the bird to explain, the bird softly says, "May I ask what the turkey did?"

LIFE LESSON

Fear is an effective tool for getting our attention and influencing our behavior. That's why it's used so frequently as a motivator by politicians, doctors, advertisers, and others. Psychologists call this *fear appeal*.

But the truth is that fear rarely inspires lasting change, and showing people the consequences of their actions doesn't usually "scare them straight" for long. So if you really want to modify your life (or someone else's), don't stop at scare tactics. Make sure you also have a positive goal and a clear plan to achieve it (see Joke 1).

BEYOND THE PUNCH LINE

Here are four key things you should know about fear appeal.

1. It works best when it's used to promote a one-time behavior (rather than a repeated behavior), such as getting a blood test or a flu shot, or a financial review.

2. A 2016 review of fifty years of scientific studies shows that for some reason, it works better on women than on men.

3. An effective fear appeal can prime someone to act. But little will happen unless the appeal also offers a viable solution, and the solution seems adequate to address the problem. In addition, objections (price, skills, beliefs) have to be anticipated and addressed in advance.

4. You need just the right amount of fear to make it work. A strong feeling of fear is more effective than a moderate one—but there's a catch: If the appeal arouses too much fear, people are likely to get defensive and go into denial. Or they may

become immobilized and panicky, and not get the message at all. On the other hand, if the appeal doesn't inspire enough fear, people tend to ignore the message entirely.

67

Dumb and Dumber

"First learn the meaning of what you say, and then speak."
—**Epictetus**

A young ventriloquist was performing at a club in a small town. He was halfway through a run of "dumb blonde" jokes when a blonde woman in the audience suddenly stood up and shouted, "I've had just about enough of your degrading jokes. Where do you get off stereotyping women that way? A person's physical attributes have *nothing* to do with their value as human beings. Guys like you keep women from being respected and from reaching their full potential because you promote discrimination against not only blondes but women in general. And why? Just for a few cheap laughs."

Stunned, the ventriloquist started to apologize, but the blonde interrupted him and shouted, "Stay out of this, mister. I'm talking to that little jerk on your knee!"

LIFE LESSON

With apologies to blondes everywhere, the lesson of this joke is: Before you express a point of view, know what you're talking about. It doesn't do any good to be totally wrong at the top of your lungs. Not only will you fail to make your point, you might end up making the other guy's. And choose your words carefully. "Your words are a reflection of who you are," explains Dr. Shirley Vandersteen. "If your words are getting you into trouble, you're showing others the very worst parts of you." So be passionate about your ideas and speak up for yourself. But before you do, have a clue.

BEYOND THE PUNCH LINE

Ever hear the phrase "Don't let your mouth write checks that your butt can't cash?" If that's your problem, here are two tricks for getting it under control.

1. Dr. Vandersteen has a simple solution: "Diligently practice closing your mouth as soon as you open it. I'm not kidding. If you have this problem, it means that you are reacting to the people and situations around you by opening your mouth and talking. You are not reacting by thinking. When you close your mouth, you are breaking the pattern or habit and taking control. You are giving yourself time to consciously *choose* what you want to say."

2. We found this clever approach in an online anxiety support forum. (Really.) The commenter calls it his Two and a Half Method. He says: "First, I consciously count to two before even thinking of a reply. When I do, I let the reply drift in my mind

to see how it emotionally fits with the conversation. Normally it mutates while it's drifting, and then comes out as something better. I don't know why it works. It just does.

"Then I deliberately say half as much. What I *do* say comes across as considered, like my words were chosen especially for that conversation. Other people will listen to you—your patience will be rewarded."

—— 68 ——

On Target

"I only believe in statistics that I doctored myself."
—Winston S. Churchill

Three guys—a politician, an economist, and a statistician—go out hunting. Moving silently through the woods, they spot a deer.

The politician hoists his rifle, takes aim, fires . . . and misses five feet to the left.

The economist scoffs, takes aim, fires . . . and misses five feet to the right.

The statistician jumps up jubilantly and yells, "We got 'im!"

LIFE LESSON

We're inundated with statistics every day—and we simply accept them as truth. But just because they sound authoritative doesn't mean they're accurate—they can be skewed, one-sided, or just outright lies.

So does that mean all stats are false? Of course not. The challenge is to listen critically, be appropriately skeptical, and then draw *your own* conclusions.

BEYOND THE PUNCH LINE

Here are a few tips on how to spot misleading statistics:

• **Check the math.** Before you examine the facts, just look at the numbers. It seems crazy, but percentages in charts or graphs sometimes add up to more (or less) than 100 percent—and no one notices.

• **Use your BS radar.** Thanks to the Internet, there are plenty of made-up statistics floating around. So if a stat seems dubious, it probably is. Keep your eyes on the numbers; misleading stats often seem correct only because we want them to be.

• **Ask yourself what's been left out.** It's very easy to create convincing half-truths by cherry-picking information that fits an agenda (see Joke 32). Colgate once advertised that 80 percent of dentists recommended their toothpaste. The implication was that only 20 percent of dentists recommended anything else. But, in fact, the surveyed dentists were allowed to pick several brands, not just one—which Colgate "forgot" to mention.

• **Consider the source.** Statistics can be manipulated to prove just about anything, so one of the first things to check is who's putting out the information, and what are they trying to prove? For example, stats about smoking might "prove" that cigarettes are either benign or lethal, depending on whether the source is the American Cancer Society or the American Tobacco Institute. Who would you believe?

• **Look carefully at the language used.** Stats are often modified by *weasel words*—"words or statements that are intentionally ambiguous or misleading." These turn legitimate stats into meaningless half-truths. For example, there may be *up to* four hundred people looking over your shoulder right now. The implication is that four hundred is a meaningful number, but, in fact, it means nothing because any number less than four hundred would be true—including zero. Other weasely expressions include "some people say," "as many as," "it's been said that, . . ." and a *zillion* (also a weasel word) more.

Too Late

"My one regret in life is that I am not someone else."
—Woody Allen

How'd you break your leg?" asked the doctor.

"Well, twenty-five years ago . . ."

"No, I'm asking how you broke your leg *this morning*."

"I'm trying to tell you, Doc. As I was saying . . . twenty-five years ago I was driving down a country road late at night and needed a place to stay. I saw a farmhouse, so I stopped and knocked on the door. I told the farmer my situation, and he let me stay in his spare bedroom. In the middle of the night, the farmer's beautiful daughter woke me up and asked if I needed anything. 'No,' I said, 'I'm fine.' She came right up next to me and asked, 'Are you sure you don't need anything?' I said, 'Yes, I'm sure.' She came even closer and whispered in my ear, 'Isn't there *something* I can do for you?' I told her, 'No, I reckon not.'"

"What does all this have to do with your broken leg?"

"Well, this morning while I was working on my house, it suddenly dawned on me what she meant . . . and I fell off the roof."

LIFE LESSON

In numerous studies, older people tell interviewers that it's not the things they *did* in life they regret—it's the things they *didn't* do. They say that opportunities show up randomly in life . . . and if you don't take advantage of them, they're gone forever. Of course, you can't do everything—you have to be selective. But if something really compelling comes along and appeals to you in a profound way, grab it. The choice may be something you remember—or regret—for the rest of your life.

BEYOND THE PUNCH LINE

What are the things you're most likely to regret? Here are five of the things older and dying people identify:

1. **"Living the life other people expected, rather the one I wanted to."** People push you to do things *they* want you to do—often saying it's "for your own good." But you have your own dreams, and if you don't pursue them, you'll regret it. Don't live for other people's dreams—follow your own. This seems to be the number-one regret at the end of life.

2. **"Not appreciating my loved ones more."** Our relationships with kids, parents, and friends make up some of life's richest experiences. But we tend to take them for granted. Don't do it. Express your love whenever and however you can.

3. **"Not being genuine."** Folk wisdom says it this way: "Be what you is and not what you ain't. 'Cause if you ain't what you is, you is what you ain't." At the end of life, people who realize they suppressed their own thoughts and feelings, and tried to be someone they weren't, experience a powerful regret.

4. **"Losing touch with friends."** Maintaining old friendships turns out to be a lot more important than you might think. At the end of life, people deeply regret "not giving friendships the time and effort that they deserve," writes Bronnie Ware in *The Top Five Regrets of the Dying*. "Everyone misses their friends when they are dying."

5. **"Spending too much time working."** Sounds like a cliché, but it turns out to be true. Work may seem pressing and important in the moment, but in the long run, it's not nearly as important as the more fulfilling things it can keep you from doing—spending time with the people and activities you love.

—— **70** ——

Thanks, But No Thanks

"I used to think the worst thing in life was to end up alone. It's not. The worst thing in life is ending up with people who make you feel alone."
—**Robin Williams**

A young man is walking through the woods, when he comes upon a bunch of old-timers sitting around a campfire. He says hello and they invite him to join the group. After a few moments of silence, one of the old-timers says, "Number seventeen." They all start laughing. The next guy says, "Number sixty-four," and again everyone starts laughing.

The young man turns to the old fellow next to him and says, "What's everybody laughing about?"

The old guy says, "Well, we've all known each other for so long that we don't need to *tell* our jokes anymore—we just refer to them by a number."

So when it's his turn, the young man stands up and says, "Number thirty-three." Nobody laughs. Embarrassed, the young man sits down and says to the guy next to him, "I don't get it. Isn't number thirty-three funny?"

"Yeah," says the old guy, "but not the way *you* tell it."

LIFE LESSON

We all learn this one the hard way: You can't fit in everywhere. Some social groups will exclude you, no matter how badly you want in or how hard you try. But don't take it as a personal failure; you can't be everyone's friend. And frankly, it may not have anything to do with you.

If you think about it, you may also find that you and your friends unintentionally (or intentionally) do the same thing to other people. You have your own taste, language, style, and it can be hard for an "outsider" to connect with you. So rather than feeling bad about where you don't belong, try taking an appreciative look at the places you *do* fit in—or keep looking until you find the group that works for you.

BEYOND THE PUNCH LINE

You might feel rejected when you try to fit in and fail. But fitting in isn't all it's cracked up to be, and the experience can be an opportunity to learn more about yourself.

• **Use rejection to reexamine your priorities.** What's really important to you? When older people are asked what they regret in life (see Joke 69), one of the most common answers is trying to please others rather than being true to themselves. "You don't want to change yourself just to fit in with a certain group of people," writes one expert. "That's where many people go wrong. They try to gain approval from others and end up losing themselves in the process."

• **Use it to appreciate what makes you different.** When you're trying to fit in, the last thing you want to hear is that you're different. But you can turn that from an indictment to an opportunity for self-discovery. Maybe your values *are* different. Or your aesthetic sense. Or your sense of humor. You could try to change these things, or you could stop trying to fit in and instead find people who appreciate you for who you are—where you don't have to be a different person to be accepted.

• **Use it to refocus your energy.** Take the energy you've been putting into trying to be accepted and channel it into your own life instead. Get clear about your personal goals and use that energy to go after what you really want. What's your dream? What haven't you done yet? This experience may be the perfect catalyst to get you moving.

71

Don't Count on It

"Change is the law of life. And those who look only to the past or present are certain to miss the future."
—**John F. Kennedy**

A man sitting at a bar let out a heavy sigh as he sipped his drink. The bartender heard him and asked, "What's wrong?"

"My great-grandpa died two weeks ago," the man replied.

"Gee, that's too bad," said the bartender.

"Well, he left me a hundred grand in his will."

"Oh, that's actually pretty good," said the bartender, a bit confused.

"I guess," said the man. "But then last week my great-uncle died and left me two hundred grand."

"Wow!" exclaimed the bartender. "So why are you so sad?"

The man looked up mournfully and said, "So far this week—not a cent!"

LIFE LESSON

When something in your life suddenly changes—for better or worse—it starts to warp your point of view: You start to think and act like it's the new normal. But most likely it's not, and it can be self-destructive to take the change too seriously. If you're having a run of good luck, enjoy it while it lasts. If you're having a run of bad luck, don't take it to heart. Either way, you can be sure that before long, it's all going to change again.

BEYOND THE PUNCH LINE

The process of change can be uncomfortable—and scary—because we know where we've been, but not where we're going. Getting used to it takes some adjustment, which we experience as a gray period called *transition*. Experts say there are three distinct stages to it:

1. The "Holy crap, I don't want to do this" stage. (We resist it.)

2. The "Hmm, this could be interesting" stage. (We consider new possibilities.)

And finally,

3. The "What change? Did something change?" stage. (We accept it.)

Of course, it would it be more convenient to just skip steps 1 and 2 and go right to acceptance. Except, as one psychologist points out, "We just don't work that way." She adds: "But by *understanding* how change works, you won't misinterpret your discomfort as a sign of trouble or a wrong move. You'll simply say—'Oh right, this is just how change is supposed to feel right now.'"

72

All About Me

"A watched pot is the only pot that boils."
—Steve Javna

A widow decides to visit the funeral home to view her husband's body before the funeral. But when she sees him laid out in a blue suit, she gets upset. "My husband was supposed to be buried in a brown suit, not a blue one," she complains to the funeral director.

The funeral director smiles and says, "Of course. We'll be glad to change it for you, madam."

The widow is satisfied, and hands him a check to cover the cost of a new suit. "Will this be sufficient?" she asks.

The funeral director smiles and replies, "Yes, that's very generous, madam."

As she's leaving the funeral home, the widow apologizes for being difficult; the funeral director smiles and says, "We understand, and we will take care of it for you, madam."

As soon as the door shuts, and the widow is out of earshot, he turns around and yells, "Hey, Ed! Switch the heads in caskets two and four!"

LIFE LESSON

Don't assume that people care about the things that matter to you—even if they smile warmly and say they do. It's not that everyone is only out for themselves—it's just that people tend to be self-involved, so your needs are not their priority. And, as our father used to say, "When people don't care, they take the easy way out . . . if they think they can get away with it." So don't let them get away with it. Be very specific about what you want, stick up for yourself, and stay involved until you're satisfied with the results.

BEYOND THE PUNCH LINE

If you have to get someone to take your concerns seriously, here are four strategies to try:

1. **Appeal to their self-interest.** Show them how helping you will benefit them.

2. **Educate them.** Explain *why* you want something done and provide context. If they see the problem through your eyes, they may be able to relate to it as if it was their own challenge.

3. **Show them what it will accomplish.** We all want to do things that matter. If helping you results in success that also raises their self-esteem, your job can give them a sense of meaning and purpose.

4. **Reach them emotionally.** Enthusiasm is contagious. When you share your excitement with other people, they get excited as well.

You still have to stay on guard—some people are good at faking emotion, and they use that as a buffer to avoid dealing with your needs. Unfortunately, if none of these things work, there's probably no way to reach them. (OK, you can yell at them. That might work.)

—— 73 ——

You May Already Be a Winner

"If I ever go looking for my heart's desire again,
I won't look any further than my own backyard.
Because if it isn't there, I never really lost it to begin with."
—Dorothy, in *The Wizard of Oz* (1939)

An American was visiting a Mexican fishing village one day when a small boat came in with several large tuna. The American asked the fisherman how long it took to catch them.

"Not long," the fisherman replied.

So why didn't he stay out longer and catch more fish, the American asked.

"No need," the fisherman replied. "I bring in enough to support my family."

"What do you do with the rest of your time?" asked the American.

"I sleep late," said the fisherman. "I fish a little, play with my children, take a siesta, spend time with my wife, and in the evening I walk into town to drink beers and sing songs with my friends. I have a good life, señor."

The American rolled his eyes. "Well, maybe, but if you spent more time fishing, you could sell the fish and use the extra money to buy a bigger boat and catch even more fish. With the proceeds from those fish, you could buy more boats. Eventually you could have a fleet, then sell your fish directly to a processor, and eventually open your own cannery. You would be vertically integrated, controlling the product, processing, and distribution. Soon you could leave this village and move to Mexico City or Los Angeles to run your empire."

"And what then, señor?"

"You go public," said the American. "You issue an IPO and sell stock in your company. You'll make a fortune!"

"A fortune, señor? What then?"

"Then," said the American, "you can retire and move to a small fishing village, where you can sleep late, fish a little, play with your children, take a siesta, spend time with your wife, and in the evening walk into town to drink beers and sing songs with your friends."

LIFE LESSON

It's conventional wisdom in our culture that you should always be reaching for more, and that having more will somehow lead to greater happiness. But you don't have to buy into that. Ask yourself: Are you satisfied with who you are and what you're doing? If you are, you've already won; it's okay to walk away from the table.

BEYOND THE PUNCH LINE

The fisherman in the joke knew instinctively what he needed in life, but a lot of us don't. If *you* still "can't get no satisfaction," researchers have some suggestions about what to focus on:

• **A strong social network.** Studies show that the main indicator for whether people are satisfied with their lives is the number of close friends and family connections they have. So although maintaining relationships takes work, it's really worth it.

• **An appreciation of your personal history.** According to researchers, people who write down their life stories are happier with their lives. Bonus: Studies indicate that knowing their family's history will boost your kids' self-esteem too.

• **Reasonable goals.** This comes up fairly frequently in studies: People who set ambitious—but attainable—goals are far more likely to be content. For example: walk a mile every day, read a book, clean the garage (see Joke 1).

• **The feeling that you're making a difference.** Research shows that people who volunteer not only enjoy their lives more, they're actually healthier and live longer.

• **A way to grow.** Psychologists say that keeping an open mind contributes to a greater sense of hopefulness and vitality.

This includes anything from taking classes to simply trying to understand another person's point of view.

• **Time to enjoy life's small pleasures.** If you can be "in the moment," you're more likely to feel centered and peaceful. Try this: For one moment, close your eyes and forget about your worries, and focus instead on where you are right now. That little bit of "mindfulness meditation" is a powerful tool in increasing your life satisfaction. The more you do it, the better you'll feel.

74

Model Behavior

"When people are free to do as they please,
they usually imitate each other."
—Eric Hoffer

Grandpa recently turned one hundred. That was a pretty big deal in our little town, so the local newspaper sent a reporter to cover his birthday party. After Grandpa blew out the candles, the reporter went over to him and asked, "Excuse me, sir. What would you say is the secret to living so long?"

"Well," said Grandpa, "the main thing is never to argue with anyone."

"*What?*" exclaimed the reporter, "Really? Not a healthy diet or regular exercise, or something like that? You're seriously asking me to believe that the secret to living to a hundred is 'never argue'? That's ridiculous!"

Grandpa thought for a moment and said, "You know, you could be right."

LIFE LESSON

Sometimes the only way to convince someone is to show them what you mean—to model behavior instead of just talking about it. In fact, that's one of the primary ways humans learn. Studies have shown that human children do something no other primate does: imitate every action of their primary adult models, regardless of whether it makes sense or not. So if your verbal message isn't getting through, remember that you can always make your point—and maybe make it better—by walking your talk and being a role model.

BEYOND THE PUNCH LINE

A ton of scientific research supports the theory that learning from modeled behavior works—in fact, a whole school of therapy is built around it. *Behavioral therapy*, developed in the late 1960s, has proven that humans can overcome many problems just by watching other people deal with them successfully. It has also demonstrated that modeling works better under certain conditions, so if you want to be a role model, keep these rules in mind:

1. The behavior you want others to copy should be presented clearly and concisely. Leave out unnecessary details—they're distracting.

2. Start with the simplest level of behavior and gradually work up to the harder parts.

3. Skill counts. The better you are at something, the more effective you'll be at modeling it. So make sure you really know what you're doing.

4. Smile! Friendly, accessible models are the most effective teachers. It also helps if the person who's modeling is the same sex and age as the observer.

5. Verify that your "student" is really getting something out of the lesson. Modeling should also include an immediate, clear reward for the behavior. This helps move a person from observing to taking action . . . which is, after all, the ultimate goal.

75

A Fish Story

"Many men go fishing all of their lives without knowing that it is not fish they are after."
—Henry David Thoreau

A Vermonter gets drunk and decides to go ice fishing. He grabs his fishing rod and his sitting bucket and heads out onto the ice. As he takes out his saw to cut a hole in the ice, he suddenly hears a tremendous booming voice from above: "YOU'LL FIND NO FISH THERE."

Stunned, the man looks around, but can't figure out where the voice is coming from. He scratches his head for a moment and then resumes cutting a hole in the ice. Again he hears the thunderous voice from above: "YOU'LL FIND NO FISH THERE."

Now the man is really rattled. He looks up and cries, "Is that you, Lord?"

"NO," the voice replies, "THIS IS THE MANAGER OF THE SKATING RINK."

LIFE LESSON

Without getting into theology, there's a practical lesson here for everyone: Not every voice that seems like the "divine" really is. Sometimes it's just a guy with a microphone.

BEYOND THE PUNCH LINE

You be the judge: Were these divine voices . . . or just guys with microphones?

• **George King.** In 1955, King founded the Aetherius Society, whose adherents believe that alien beings he called "Cosmic Masters" control the fate of man and that the Messiah will arrive in a flying saucer.

• **Hogen Fukunaga.** In 1987, Fukunaga created *Ho No Hana Sanpogyo*, known as "the foot-reading cult." His 30,000 followers believed he was the reincarnation of Jesus and Buddha, and could diagnose people's problems by examining the soles of their feet.

• **Claude Vorilhon.** A French racecar driver who, in 1974, changed his name to Raël and founded the Raëlian movement. Their primary tenet: Human beings were created by a race of aliens called Elohim.

• **Hon-Ming Chen.** He founded the Chen Tao (True Way) cult, whose core principles include the belief that every human has three souls and that our solar system was created by a nuclear war. He famously predicted that God would appear on all North American TV sets at 12:01 a.m. on March 31, 1998.

—— 76 ——

Helping Hands

*"When you know what a man wants
you know who he is, and how to move him."*
—George R.R. Martin

A man was sent to prison for armed robbery. After a few months, he received a letter from his father.

Dear Son: It looks like I won't be able to plant the potato garden this year. I hate to miss it, but I guess I'm just too old to be digging up a garden plot by myself. If you were here, I know you'd do it for me. As it is, there's not much I can do. Hope you are well. Love, Dad

Shortly after, the old man received a letter from his son: "For God's sake, Dad, don't dig up the garden! That's where I buried the money!"

A few days later, a gang of FBI agents appeared at the house and proceeded to dig up the entire garden ... without finding any money. Confused, the father wrote another letter to his son telling him what had happened. "What should I do?" he asked.

His son's reply: "*Now* plant your potatoes."

LIFE LESSON

When you're trying to accomplish something, there are times when you have to be especially creative in using the resources available to you. One of those resources is people.

If you understand people and can figure out what they're already inclined to do—especially if it's something that will make them feel good about themselves or their jobs—you can turn them into your allies without their even knowing it. Good managers do this all the time without making employees feel abused or taken advantage of. They know that the right tasks will give people a sense of fulfillment, and they'll want to do more.

BEYOND THE PUNCH LINE

Here are six ideas about how to get people to help you do your work:

1. **Do something for them first.** Offer to help them *before* you need them. When you want help, don't make it a quid pro

quo—keep the two jobs separate. They'll make the connection without your having to bring it up.

2. Ask for a big favor—one you know will be rejected. Then go back and ask for a smaller one—the one you really wanted all along. Researchers call this *the door in the face* approach and they've found it actually works. The person who said no will likely feel guilty for having turned you down and make amends by helping with the smaller, more reasonable favor.

3. Make it sound exciting. Enthusiasm is contagious. If you're excited about your task, potential helpers are more likely to be too. Let them know that you're doing it regardless of whether you get help, but because it's going to be a really big thing you want to include them. If they say no, don't be deterred. Maybe they'll join next time . . . and you can always ask someone else.

4. Ask someone who's helped you on another job. Fund-raisers know that the person most likely to contribute money is someone who's contributed before. The same is true here. They're already part of your team, so they're primed to help.

5. Validate the other person. Make them feel good about the work they're doing for you. Research shows that flattery works—but only if it's personal and sincere. If you like their attitude, their ideas, their energy, or anything else about their behavior, tell them.

6. Praise them—publicly and privately. Saying thank you is the least expensive gift you can give—and it can have almost as much effect as the most expensive one. Interestingly, the opposite is also true: Failing to thank someone who has helped you makes them feel unappreciated, and they'll probably never help you again.

—— 77 ——

Reach Out

*"Let wise men be wise by instinct if they can,
but when this fails, be wise by good advice."*
—**Sophocles**

A woman runs into a doctor's office and pleads, "Doctor! Doctor! Please help me! Everywhere I touch on my body it hurts!"

The doctor is quite concerned and says, "Of course. Show me."

So the woman pokes her ankle and screams in pain. Then she pokes her knee and screams in pain. Then she pokes her forehead and screams again.

The doctor stops her. "That's enough," he says. "Let me think this over." He ponders in silence for a moment, and proclaims, "Okay, I know what the problem is. You broke your finger."

LIFE LESSON
Feeling stressed out or in pain? In situations like that, it's hard to think clearly . . . and easy to jump to false conclusions. So although it may not be your first impulse, that's an excellent

time to reach out and ask for advice. Someone who's objective might have the expertise—or just the common sense—to see what you can't. And you might be surprised at how simple the solution to your problem really is.

BEYOND THE PUNCH LINE

Ready to ask for advice? Here's ours:

1. **Don't be afraid to ask.** Contrary to what you might expect, studies show that asking for advice doesn't make people think you're lazy or incompetent—it actually makes you look smarter to them. They're likely to take your request for assistance as a compliment and give you extra credit for going to *them* instead of someone less knowledgeable. The result is that you gratify their ego, get the information you need, and build a relationship all at the same time.

2. **Ask specific questions.** Do your homework *before* approaching someone for advice. Make an effort to answer each question yourself, then ask pointed questions to fill in the remaining gaps in your knowledge. If you show the "adviser" what you do know, they'll be happy to help you with what you don't.

3. **Ask one general question.** After you've gotten answers to your questions, ask one final, general question such as, "Is there anything else that I need to know?" or "Do you have any other suggestions?" Now that the adviser has a sense of what you're looking for, they may be able to provide additional information—something, perhaps, you never even thought to ask.

78

Didn't Step in It

"Sometimes the cure is worse than the disease."
—**Yiddish proverb**

Two girls are walking down the street. One stops suddenly and points at the ground in horror. She says, "Is that dog poop?"

The other girl eyes it warily. Then she puts her nose right up to it. "It smells like dog poop."

Both girls stick their fingers in it. The first girl says, "And it feels like dog poop."

They both put their fingers in their mouths. The second girl says, "Yeah, and it tastes like dog poop."

"Phew!" says the first girl. "Sure glad we didn't step in it."

LIFE LESSON

Yes, this is an elementary school joke. But both of us really use it: We often invoke the punch line ("Sure glad I didn't step in it") when we realize that by trying to avoid something, we've actually made matters worse. It reminds us that sometimes it's smarter to take a risk and deal with the consequences than it is to sidestep something that isn't much of a threat in the first place. To put it another way: Stepping in s**t is no fun . . . but it's still better than eating it.

BEYOND THE PUNCH LINE

How do you tell when taking a risk is reasonable and when it's foolish? Here are three questions to ask when you're doing a "personal risk analysis."

1. **How likely is it that things will go wrong?** According to the widely accepted Prospect Theory, we're more inclined to focus on potential loss than on potential gain when analyzing risk. Anticipating loss triggers a fight-or-flight response in our nervous systems: The heart beats faster and more cortisol is released, which makes it hard to think straight. As a result, we tend to exaggerate the prospect of real risk. For a more balanced view, flip your thought process and also ask, "What if it all goes *right*?" As Mark Twain said, "I am an old man and have known a great many troubles, but most of them never happened."

2. **If problems arise, can you deal with them?** A study in the *Journal of Consumer Research* indicates that most of us start off with an inflated view of our skills, but as soon as we encounter difficulties, our judgment reverses and we *underestimate* our ability to handle them. Studies suggest that in a crisis, we're more capable than we believe. So are you *over*estimating or *under*estimating yourself?

3. **How bad could it really be? Define your worst-case scenario.** Compare that with what it will take to avoid the potential risk. You may find that the outcome you fear most isn't actually so bad. And if you've got a plan B (see Joke 34), it will be even less threatening.

79

Orange You Sorry?

*"At any street corner the feeling of absurdity
can strike any man in the face."*
—Albert Camus

A man with a big orange head goes to see a doctor. The doctor is amazed. "My God," he says, "how did this happen?"

"Well, it's a long story," the man replies. "A few years ago I was walking along the beach when I stubbed my toe on something. I looked down and saw an antique brass lantern. So I picked it up and brushed off the sand … and suddenly a genie popped out. In a thunderous voice he said, 'You have released me from my prison, and in gratitude I will grant you three wishes.' I said, 'OK, I'd like to be fantastically wealthy.' 'Granted,' the genie said, and an instant later I had a wallet full of cash and a briefcase full of stocks and bonds. So then I said, 'I want to be irresistibly attractive to beautiful women.' 'Granted,' said the genie, and an instant later three supermodels appeared out of nowhere and draped themselves all over me. Then the genie said, 'What is your third wish?'—and you know, this may be where I went wrong, because I said, 'I'd like a big orange head.'"

LIFE LESSON

This is what's known as an "anti-joke." It doesn't have a punch line like other jokes. There's no slapstick or wordplay, and it's probably not going to make you go "HA-HA." But not all humor does. What's funny about this joke is that it's absurd. It embraces what one sociologist calls "the condition of existing in a meaningless and irrational world."

That should sound at least a little familiar to everyone. Despite our best efforts to find meaning in life, there are invariably times when things just don't make sense. You *could* let them upset you, but why not laugh at them instead? This isn't surrender. In fact, the opposite is true—seeing humor in an absurd situation is both sublime and empowering. Try it.

BEYOND THE PUNCH LINE

Intrigued by absurd humor? So are we. Here are four quick anti-jokes to . . . enjoy?

1. Roses are gray. Violets are gray. I am a dog.

2. Two elephants were flying—one to the north, and the red one.

3. Two bear cubs are in the bathroom. One turns to the other and says, "Could you pass the toilet paper?" The other bear says, "What do I look like, a typewriter?"

4. Deepest, darkest jungle. Heat and humidity thick as molasses. In a clearing is a small pool of water where two hippopotamuses are seeking refuge from the heat. One turns to the other and says, "You know . . . I just can't get it through my head that this is Thursday."

80

Don't Take It Personally

"Criticism is something we can avoid easily by saying nothing, doing nothing, and being nothing."
—Aristotle

Tony was training to be a boxer. He weighed 215 pounds and had a solid, muscular build, but he just wasn't a very good fighter. Finally, his trainer got fed up and lit into him. "I don't get it, Tony. You're huge and fast, but you punch like an old lady and you can't block to save your life. Why, if I was your size, I'd be the heavyweight champion of the world!"

"Really?" replied Tony. "So how come you're not the lightweight champion of the world?"

LIFE LESSON

Before you accept someone's criticism, take a careful look at where it's coming from. Look at their motives. Is the critic trying to help you . . . or put you down? There's a lot to learn from thoughtful criticism, but it's not necessary to take every critique seriously. Be selective about what (and whom) you listen to, and don't hesitate to brush off criticism that doesn't apply to you.

BEYOND THE PUNCH LINE

Three simple questions to ask when someone starts criticizing:

1. Do you care what this person says or thinks about you? If not, forget about it.

2. Is the criticism constructive? Constructive criticism is meant to help you. It offers realistic suggestions for improvement, things you can actually do, and respects who you are. It's what you expect from friends.

3. Is the criticism destructive? Destructive criticism is an attack. It diminishes you and lowers your self-esteem. You may still be able to learn something from it, but only if you can filter out the negativity. Keep your guard up; don't let people who want to hurt you get into your head.

Experts suggest a few basic rules for dealing with criticism:

• **Don't take it personally.** Remember that it's just someone sharing their observations or opinion; it's not divine judgment.

• **Stay calm and rational.** Keep it together—particularly if you're at work. Save your outrage for later, when you're with friends.

• **Don't make excuses.** If it's valid criticism, don't rebut it— just listen. You can't hear what critics are saying if you're busy defending yourself. Plus, people get tired of being interrupted and may just give up. Then you lose the benefit of their insights.

• **Listen for the real message.** Even if it's painful, listen for the guidance they're providing. What's the grain of truth? What can you learn?

• **Don't forget to say thanks.** It pays to cultivate a network of helpful critics. Personal growth often depends on getting thoughtful feedback from friends.

––––– 81 –––––

I Won't Grow Up

"You can only be young once.
But you can always be immature."
—**Dave Barry**

At one point during a Little League game, the coach calls one of his young players over to his side. "Tommy, do you understand what a team is and what cooperation is?" The little boy nods yes.

"Okay. And do you understand that what really matters is that we win together, as a team?" Again, the boy nods yes.

"And when the umpire calls a strike or calls you out at first base," says the coach, "we don't curse or attack the umpire. Do you understand all that, Tommy?" Once again the little boy nods yes.

"Great," says the coach. "Now go over and explain it to your mother."

LIFE LESSON

There's a real phenomenon called "Little League syndrome." It refers to parents who get so emotionally involved with their kids' competitive sports that they become verbally abusive—and sometimes even violent—at games. But Little League syndrome doesn't just apply to baseball. You can encounter it anywhere. Temper tantrums, poor impulse control, etc.—behaviors that are normal for children—are a warning sign of immaturity in adults. These people require special handling, so if you're not prepared to invest time and energy dealing with them, walk away—even if you really like them.

BEYOND THE PUNCH LINE

How do you know when it's time to walk away? Look for these red flags:

• **Self-centeredness.** Psychologists say it's the main personality trait of immature adults. They need to be the center of attention, no matter how it affects other people.

• **Name calling.** Children use it to assert power and to cover up fear and insecurity. So do immature adults.

• **Crybaby behavior.** They constantly complain and refuse to be satisfied with anything.

• **Blaming.** They get defensive, make excuses, and blame other people for what they've done.

• **Lying.** They lie to stay out of trouble, just like young children.

Experts suggest that you treat immature adults like children. Give them limits, set standards of acceptable behavior, and establish consequences for bad behavior. For example:

• **If they start griping, change the subject.**

• **If they're acting out, don't take the bait.** Giving them attention makes things worse. Don't react—wait until they finish; then try talking. If they keep it up, excuse yourself and calmly walk away.

• **And finally, consider keeping your emotional distance.** Even if you have to be around them, you don't have to invest in the relationship. They can be very toxic.

82

SAY *WHAT*?

*"The single biggest problem in communication
is the illusion that it has taken place."*
—George Bernard Shaw

After years of pouring his heart out to his therapist, investing countless hours and a substantial part of his income in the sessions, a man finally works up enough courage to ask a question about a puzzling part of his therapist's method that he's never understood.

"Doctor," says the patient, "I've been coming to you once a week for five years, sharing all the painful details of my childhood, exposing all my insecurities, recounting all my regrets, and sobbing about my difficult personal relationships. And all the while, you've sat there, listening and observing, but never once asking a question or offering advice. Why? Why the silence?"

The therapist nods thoughtfully, looks down at his notes, and finally after a long pause, says, "No hablo Inglés."

LIFE LESSON

At face value, it may seem preposterous that someone could spend years in an intimate relationship and then suddenly discover they haven't been communicating. But it happens all the time. Think about it: How many times have you assumed that a friend understood exactly what you were telling them, only to find out much later that they'd gotten it completely wrong—or weren't really listening in the first place? Studies show that we consistently assume people understand what we mean—even when there's no good reason to do so—because it's comforting to believe we're not alone and others see the world as we do. One consequence: We tend to place trust in people who haven't earned it.

BEYOND THE PUNCH LINE

Successful relationships—whether in business, friendship, or love—depend on good verbal communication. And the easiest way to find out if your words are getting through to someone is simply to ask them. Personal coaches call it a *communications feedback loop*, but there's nothing complicated about it: You just ask a question that requires a response, such as "What do you think?" Or you can ask the listener to repeat what they heard you say, in their own words. By doing this, you're allowing the other person to actively participate, and giving both of you a chance to establish a trusting relationship—or not.

83

First Time Around

"They may forget what you said,
but they will never forget how you made them feel."
—Carl W. Buehner

T he new CEO of a large company wanted to shake
things up and made it clear that ridding the
company of slackers was a priority. On his first
day, while touring company headquarters, he walked into
a room full of workers and noticed one young guy just
standing around, leaning against a wall. Eager to make a
memorable first impression and show the rest of the team
he was serious, he went over to the guy and asked, "How
much do you make here?"

"I make $250 a week," the guy replied. "Why?"

The CEO pulled out $1,000 in cash, handed it to the guy,
and shouted, "Here's a month's pay. Take it and get out!
AND DON'T COME BACK!"

Satisfied that he'd shown his employees who was
boss, the CEO looked around the room and said, "Does
anyone know what that screwup did here?"

After a long pause, someone in the back of the room
finally answered, "He's the pizza delivery guy."

LIFE LESSON

First impressions set the tone for the future of a relationship. Studies show that if people are positively impressed when they first meet you, they'll open up and want more contact. But if you make a bad impression, they're less likely to trust you. When you know you're going to meet people for the first time, prepare for it. If you go in unprepared, there's a good chance you'll look foolish . . . and you may never get that opportunity again.

BEYOND THE PUNCH LINE

Research has shown that first impressions are formed in the first few seconds (or less) of meeting someone. And once an impression is formed, it's nearly impossible to change. Try to get the most out of those first critical moments by:

• **Paying attention to body language.** Studies show that your posture, handshake, eye contact, etc., have four times more impact on a first impression than the things you say. If you're unsure of how you come across, practice in a mirror.

• **Doing some research.** Find out everything you can about people you'll be meeting. Then pick one thing that you've learned and make a point of mentioning it in conversation. "You'll appear interesting and knowledgeable," explains one consultant, "two qualities that help make a good impression."

• **Listening attentively.** You don't have to "wow" anyone with how smart you are. Just listen to what they're saying and, in return, ask pertinent, thoughtful questions. If you're interested in them, they'll tend to trust you more.

84

Personal Pain

"No one can make you feel inferior without your consent."
—Eleanor Roosevelt

A husband and wife go into a dentist's office. The husband makes it clear to the dentist that he's in a hurry. "I need to have a tooth pulled, but I don't want any expensive extras, Doctor—no gas or novocaine. Just pull the tooth and let's get this over with as quickly as possible."

"Wow," said the dentist. "I wish more patients were as brave as you. Now, which tooth is it?"

The husband turns to his wife and says, "Open your mouth and show him, honey."

LIFE LESSON
This joke is about the need to set clear boundaries. You're the only one who knows how you feel—so when someone crosses the invisible line that marks where you begin and they end, as the husband did, it's up to you to let them know they've gone too far. You have the power to decide whom to let into your life, and how far to let them in. So use that power—don't be a victim.

BEYOND THE PUNCH LINE
Think of this as a health issue. Our physical and emotional health often depends on an ability to maintain boundaries

with others. Here are a few pointers that might make the process easier:

1. **Expect to feel guilty.** Putting limits on a relationship may bring up feelings of guilt and self-doubt. Ignore them; give yourself permission to start thinking of your own welfare. It might feel as though you're being harsh by setting boundaries, but it's not healthy to be a martyr.

2. **Experiment to find your limits.** We all have a relationship comfort zone. How do you figure out where yours is? Pay attention to how you feel in various circumstances. Experts say that two feelings in particular are tip-offs that your boundaries are being crossed: discomfort and resentment.

3. **Speak up.** No one can read your mind—you have to let others know where your boundaries are. Be direct. Explain if it's appropriate, but don't argue or feel you have to justify. If a "friend" isn't sympathetic, they may be revealing that your welfare is not their concern.

4. **Expect anger.** This may be the other person's emotional defense, or it may be an effort to control you—bullies use anger to intimidate people into compliance. Don't let their anger change your path—their anger is their problem, not yours.

5. **Be practical.** Are you emotionally prepared for pushback? If not, it may be a good strategy to start with small, nonthreatening boundaries and expand them incrementally. Creating new habits and changing behavior take consistency (see Joke 1). So whatever you decide to do, above all, follow through on it.

85

Appreciating Life

*"Life is what happens to you
while you're making other plans."*
—John Lennon

After weeks of rain, a small town was flooded and all the residents had to be evacuated from their homes. When the rescue boat came to the last house on one particular block, rescue workers found a man standing waist-deep in water in his front hallway. "C'mon! The water's rising! Get in the boat," the rescuers shouted to him.

But the man, who was deeply religious, shouted back, "NO! I have faith in God, and *He* will save me!"

Within a few hours, the floodwaters rose even higher and chased the man to the second floor of his house. Luckily, though, another rescue boat came by. "Mister, you can't stay here! The water's still rising! Get in the boat!" the rescuers shouted.

"NO WAY," the man replied. "I have faith in God, and *He* will save me!"

The floodwaters continued to rise, and soon the man had to retreat to the highest point on the roof of his house.

But fortunately, a rescue helicopter came by and dropped a ladder for the man. The pilot shouted to him through a megaphone, "Mister, PLEASE! The water's still rising! Grab the ladder and let's get out of here!"

The man steadfastly refused. "NO! I have faith in God, and *He* will save me!"

But as the floodwaters rose above the roof of the house, the man was swept away and soon drowned. When he arrived at the pearly gates, the man demanded an audience with God. "God," he said, "I was absolutely certain that you'd save me . . . but you let me die. Why? Why did you abandon me?"

God replied, "What do you mean? I sent you two boats and a helicopter!"

LIFE LESSON

Some people can only recognize a gift if it's gift-wrapped. That's a shame, because precious gifts are sitting right in front of us, in plain view—so many, in fact, that it's hard not to take them for granted. It may sound corny, but life really is much richer when we take the time to appreciate the "ordinary" things in our lives and remind ourselves—at least every once in a while—that we are surrounded by miracles.

BEYOND THE PUNCH LINE

What miraculous things do *you* take for granted? We came up with a list of fifty without even trying. But since we don't have room for fifty, here are four to start you thinking:

1. **Antibiotics.** Today a sore throat or a cut is no big deal, but for 200,000 years, human beings routinely died from infections. Antibiotics have only been in use for about 90 years—and your life may be among the 200 million they've saved.

2. **Bipedalism.** Walking on two legs has freed our arms for other tasks, like using tools, cooking, writing, etc. And because we stand instead of having our heads parallel to the ground like quadrupeds, we see more of the world. (And we can play soccer.)

3. **Clean drinking water.** Nearly a billion people worldwide don't have access to clean water. Do you? Chances are, your water is not only safe to drink, it is delivered right to your house.

4. **Wheels.** Historians estimate that the wheel was invented around 3,500 BC—but was only used for making pottery. Some three hundred years later, someone put it on a wheelbarrow. For millennia since then, wheels have been essential to human existence.

What would you include in your list? Shoes, eyes, refrigerators, toenails, aspirin, computers? Give it a shot. It may give you a new perspective on "ordinary" things.

Other People's Money

*"It's good to have money and the things that money can buy,
but it's good, too, to check up once in a while and make sure
you haven't lost the things that money can't buy."*
—George Lorimer

An old man was on his deathbed, surrounded by his wife, his three children, and his nurse. Knowing the end was near, he said to them:

"Jason, I want you to take the houses in Pacific Heights."

"Rebecca, you get the apartments in Oakwood Plaza."

"Josh, I want you to take the office building in City Center."

"And Susan, my dear wife, please take all the stores and residential buildings downtown."

Then he quietly passed away.

The nurse was impressed. She quietly went over to the wife. "I'm so sorry for your loss," she said, "but you must be very proud of your husband for having accumulated so much wealth."

"What wealth?" said the wife. "He had a paper route."

LIFE LESSON

In the modern world, it's impossible *not* to notice what other people have—or seem to have—and make assumptions about their lives. But as our father used to tell us, "Don't worry about other people's money." In the first place, you're just making it up, and like the nurse in the joke, you're probably wrong. And in the second, looking at what other people have can just be a distraction from your own life—one that probably doesn't accomplish anything other than making you feel bad (or falsely good) about yourself. Instead, stay focused on your own life, and do the best you can with it. That's what matters.

BEYOND THE PUNCH LINE

Here are five ways to change your thinking when you start to feel distracted by other people's money:

1. **Recognize that it's not about them—it's about you.** Your concern with what other people have is a sign that something in your own life needs attention. Take a closer look—ask yourself why you care what someone else has. It may help you understand what you can do to make yourself happier.

2. **Focus on what you have—not on what you think is missing.** When you start to enumerate the things you love in your life, you can appreciate how much is *right* about it, and be less concerned with what someone else has.

3. **Focus on abundance, not scarcity.** Remind yourself that there's more than enough to go around. Someone else having something doesn't prevent *you* from having something as well, and you can be glad for them without depriving yourself.

4. **Connect with your peers.** Social connection is a proven key to happiness, no matter what your economic circumstances. Surrounding yourself with people who share your values and experiences is a powerful counterbalance to envy and the distraction of materialism.

5. **Recognize that nobody has everything they want in life, but it's still your life and you love it.** As an itinerant "prophet" who called himself Brother John once "preached" to us (really):

"When someone tells you they're envious of someone else, tell them this poem:

'You've got your life and I've got mine.

But if we hung them out on the line,

You'd take yours and I'd take mine.'"

87

Payback

"Before borrowing money from a friend,
decide which you need more."
—Addison Hallock

Two guys are sitting in a bar. Suddenly, a couple of robbers walk in and shout, "This is a holdup!" As the thieves move from customer to customer relieving them of their wallets and jewelry, one of the guys slips his friend a wad of cash and whispers, "Here's that hundred I owe you."

LIFE LESSON

Everyone learns this eventually: Money changes relationships. People you'd trust for almost anything else can become unpredictable when money is involved. They might be gracious about it, or they might try to take advantage of you—there's no way to know in advance. And there are no exceptions; even the closest friendships can end over money. So should you avoid loaning it to friends and family? Probably. But if you do it anyway, be forewarned that you're putting both your relationships *and* your cash at risk.

BEYOND THE PUNCH LINE

Here are five things to keep in mind if you're thinking about loaning money to a close friend or family member:

1. **It's okay to say no.** Don't let yourself be guilt-tripped into it—it's your money, and you need to be sure you want to make the loan. If you ignore the inner voice that says "don't," you'll regret it and maybe even resent it. Be sympathetic ("I'm sorry to hear you're in a tight spot") but if you're not going to loan the money, say so as concisely and nicely as you can. A long explanation won't help. If you feel put on the spot and don't know how to get away, say you'll look over your finances and let them know.

2. **Offer to help in other ways.** If you can't—or don't want to— loan them money, you can always help them create a budget, help find credit counseling, help them find another loan source or a part-time job, or just brainstorm alternate possibilities.

3. **If you do say yes, keep it formal.** A loan is a business deal, and the whole thing can go sideways quickly if you don't treat it like one. Put the agreement in writing: What are the payment terms? Are you charging interest? How will you handle late payments? A formal deal makes it more likely the borrower will take it seriously—so you're more likely to get your money back.

4. **Stay on top of it.** You're not being unkind if you send reminders or insist on timely payments—it's the deal you made. And if a problem arises, address it right away. It's too easy for a friend to exploit your relationship and "forget" to pay—unless you make it clear that's what you expect.

5. **And finally, don't loan what you can't afford to lose.** Remember that even with a close friend or relative, there's no guarantee you're going to get your money back.

88

The Wrong Tool

*"It's so much easier to suggest solutions when
you don't know too much about the problem."*
—Malcolm Forbes

Two guys were out hunting when they got hopelessly lost. They had no compass or cell phone service, and it was getting dark. "You know," said one of the hunters, "my dad always told me that if I ever get lost, I should fire three shots into the air." So he shot three times, and they waited . . . and waited, but no rescue party came.

"Well, that didn't work," said the other hunter. "I'll try." So he shot three times into the air, and they waited . . . and waited . . . but still no rescuers came.

"Now what do we do?" moaned the first guy, "It's getting dark. And we're almost out of arrows!"

LIFE LESSON

The obvious lesson here is to use the right tool for the job. But there's a better one: Rather than blindly following instructions, take the time to be certain you understand them in the first place. And then, just to be sure, take another minute to verify that following them will actually get the job done. As the morons in the joke demonstrate, the key to selecting the right tool is understanding the problem. If you don't know what you're trying to do, you may very well find yourself shooting arrows into the air, wondering why no one is coming to rescue you.

BEYOND THE PUNCH LINE

Ever been at a meeting where the goal was to figure out how to solve a specific problem? Most people will focus on the solution, which seems logical—but it's a mistake. Research shows that the only way to really solve a problem is by addressing its root cause and figuring out why it's a problem in the first place. As Rolls-Royce chief engineer Darrell Mann puts it, "defining a problem clearly and completely represents 90 percent of the difficulty." Without understanding the root cause, your "solution" has a lower chance of success and greater chance of creating more problems.

To address this issue, Japanese automaker Toyota developed something called the "A3 Report," which has revolutionized problem-solving techniques around the world. The name refers to the size of a piece of paper in Japan—about the same size as an 11" x 17" sheet.

Here's how you can use "A3 thinking" to understand your problems: Fold the sheet of paper in half, and then unfold it. On the left side, describe your problem; on the right side, discuss what to do about it. There are no firm rules about how to structure an A3 Report, but generally on the left side you put:

• The background (or "What's happening?")

• The current situation

• Your goal

• Analysis of the problem's root cause

On the right side you put:

• Action items (possible countermeasures)

• An implementation timeline

• A plan for checking results

• Follow-up (how to verify that the problem's been solved)

Proponents of the A3 Report (and there are many) say that it tells the story of a problem in a concise and meaningful way. When you're done with the A3, you'll have a good idea of what the question is, and answers should start coming to you.

89

Enough, Already

"Some are blessed with musical ability, others with good looks. Myself, I was blessed with modesty."
—Roger Moore

Jesus and St. Peter decide to play a round of golf. St. Peter steps up to the tee on a par three. He drives the ball down the middle of the fairway, right onto the green. Jesus is up next. He slices it over the fence and into the adjacent street, where it bounces off a truck, hits the roof of an old shed, and rolls onto the ground. A squirrel runs over and tries to eat the ball. A nearby snake suddenly strikes at the squirrel and swallows it, ball and all. An eagle sees the snake and swoops down, grabs it in its talons, and flies away. As the eagle flies over the green, lightning hits it. The bird drops the snake, the snake regurgitates the squirrel, the squirrel spits out the ball, and the ball rolls into the cup, giving Jesus a hole-in-one. Exasperated, St. Peter looks over at Jesus. "Are you gonna play golf?" he asks. "Or are you just gonna fool around?"

LIFE LESSON

No matter how good you are at something, it's prudent to show a little restraint. Every situation is different, but in general, people don't appreciate being shown up. And their reaction will carry over into the way they feel about you . . . for eternity.

BEYOND THE PUNCH LINE

What are you really showing people when you show off? You may think you're just playing around, but here's what others see:

• **Insecurity.** They suspect you want their approval as a substitute for genuine self-confidence.

• **Arrogance.** They feel you're putting them down by demonstrating that somehow you're better than they are.

• **Low self-esteem.** They see you as trolling for compliments because deep down, you don't think very highly of yourself.

• **A pain in the neck.** You're demanding to be the center of attention, regardless of other people's needs.

And if you're the one who's being one-upped, here's a quick tip for how to deal with show-offs: Ignore them. Let them tell you how great their kids are, or how much money they make, or how good their golf game is. Then say, "Oh, that's terrific" . . . and walk away.

90

Thank You for Not Sharing

"Too much information can be as disconcerting as too little."
—Patricia Wentworth

Bob noticed that his friend Fred, a shopkeeper, looked upset. "What's wrong?" he asked.

"I placed an ad for a night watchman," Fred replied.

"And you didn't get any responses?" asked Bob.

"Oh, I got a response, all right. Last night someone robbed the store."

LIFE LESSON

Asking for help always makes you vulnerable in some way, because you're revealing a weakness. But be careful about how much personal information you reveal in the process; share only as much as you have to. Oversharing won't increase your chances of getting the help you need, but it might make it easier for someone to take advantage of you.

BEYOND THE PUNCH LINE

In this era of social media and reality television, oversharing is rampant—everyone knows too much about everyone else. Do you need to control *your* urge to overshare? Here are some tricks that might help you deal with it:

• **Think ahead.** Experts say oversharing is a response to feeling insecure. When you're nervously trying to impress someone with how clever and interesting you are, you're not directing enough mental energy to the filters that control what you say—and anything might pop out. So if you're going to be in a situation where you care what the other person thinks—a first date? a job interview?—anticipate the inclination to over-share, and pay extra attention to what you're saying.

• **Consider the listener.** Be realistic. Do they have the time or emotional availability to deal with a major download of your anxiety? If the answer is no, then don't share.

• **Keep your personal information personal.** Once you put it out there—especially on social media—you can't get it back. Treat it with respect; don't make yourself unnecessarily vulnerable.

• **Be careful in public.** When you're in a café or on the super-market checkout line, people really *are* listening to your conver-sations. So keep your voice down and watch what you say.

• **Think about the ripple effect.** How will family, friends, co-workers, or anyone else important to you feel if they find out you've overshared and spilled the beans about them? If they'd be upset to know you blabbed, it's a good indication that you shouldn't blab to begin with.

91

It's Not You, It's You

"Take your life in your own hands and what happens?
A terrible thing—no one is to blame."
—Erica Jong

A psychiatrist is seeing a patient for the first time. "Before we start," she says to the patient, "I want to do a few simple tests to get a better idea of what's bothering you." She reaches into a stack of cards and pulls out a picture of a square. "Tell me, what does this make you think of?" she asks. The patient grins. "That's a window," he says, "and you wouldn't believe what's going on in there!" The psychiatrist holds up a picture of a circle. "What does *this* look like to you?" she asks. The patient leers. "That's a porthole, and boy-oh-boy, what's going on in there!" The psychiatrist then pulls out a picture of a triangle. "How about this?" she asks. The patient is practically salivating now. "That's a keyhole," he gasps, "and you wouldn't believe what's going on in there!" The doctor stops and says, "I don't have to do any more tests. It's obvious that you're obsessed with sex." The patient glares back at her and says, "Me?! What about you, showing me all those dirty pictures?!"

LIFE LESSON

There's no way around it—every once in a while, you're going to run into someone who wants to blame you for *their* problems. And unless you're a therapist, it won't be a psychiatric patient—it'll be a business associate, a friend, or maybe even a family member. Don't take it personally; remember that it's their problem, not yours. And it's up to you to decide whether you want to let them engage you or not.

BEYOND THE PUNCH LINE

Avoiding victimization by a chronic blamer can be as simple as setting emotional boundaries—having a clear idea of who you are and how you feel (see Joke 84). But blamers have a negative, disruptive effect on the people around them, so it's also helpful to have strategies to deal with them.

• **Talk to them.** Most people are dumbstruck when they get blamed for something that isn't their fault. If that happens to you, force yourself to have a conversation with the blamer. Talk about their behavior and tell them how it makes you feel. You probably won't enlighten them (or you might), but you'll feel more in control of the situation.

• **Disengage.** Blamers don't make great listeners, so why torture yourself by trying to reach them, especially in the heat of a confrontation? Protect yourself. Tell them you're taking a break and simply walk away. If the other person is someone you care about, offer to return in a few minutes to talk. If not, keep walking.

• **Admit your part.** On the other hand, consider the possibility that you really did play a role in creating the situation. If, on reflection, you find that you enabled the blamer in some way, try using the moment as a vehicle for personal growth. You may not be able to fix the other person, but you might avoid repeating the situation.

—— 92 ——

I Knew It!

"Pessimism becomes a self-fulfilling prophecy;
it reproduces itself by crippling our willingness to act."
—Howard Zinn

hree turtles decided to go on a picnic. They packed a basket with sandwiches, cookies, and sodas, and set out on a ten-day journey to the picnic site. But when they reached the spot, they realized they'd forgotten to bring a bottle opener. The oldest turtle asked the youngest turtle to go back and get it. "No way," said the young one. "As soon as I go, you'll eat all the sandwiches."

The two older turtles promised they'd wait until he got back, so the young turtle agreed to go. A week went by, then a month, then a year, and the oldest turtle finally said, "Oh, he's not coming. So let's eat the sandwiches."

Suddenly, the youngest turtle popped up from behind a rock and said, *"I knew it!* I'm not going!"

LIFE LESSON

Sometimes we're so convinced something will happen that we actually make it happen. Psychologists call this a *self-fulfilling prophecy* (SFP). "Consciously or not," explains one expert, "we tip people off as to what our expectations are. We exhibit thousands of cues—some as subtle as the tilting of a head—and people pick up on those cues." Then they obligingly respond as we "expected" they would—which proves to us that we were right in the first place.

What makes a self-fulfilling prophecy so difficult to deal with is that we're almost always unaware we have a hand in it. But if we look for patterns in our lives, we'll often find a common thread that indicates we're actually making our own heaven or hell. And once we're aware of it, we can finally begin to do something about it.

BEYOND THE PUNCH LINE

Don't underestimate the power of a self-fulfilling prophecy. Studies have shown that SFPs can be powerful forces—both positive and negative—in our lives.

• In one famous 1968 experiment, a teacher was told that five of her students were exceptionally bright. Actually, their test scores were average, but because they were regarded as smart, they began to perform better—and they continued to excel throughout their lives.

• Other studies have demonstrated that excessive pessimism creates negative SFPs. In one experiment, doctors were amazed to find that when patients expected painkillers to be ineffective, their level of pain actually increased, even though the dose they were taking was clinically proven to be effective and the drugs were administered intravenously. On the other hand, subjects in the experiment who believed in the efficacy of the painkillers had a significant reduction in pain.

• This would indicate that "Fake it 'til you make it" might be good advice. By acting optimistic and confident, you may actually develop a solid belief in your ability to succeed . . . which will help you achieve your goals. Of course this doesn't always work, but there's certainly evidence that it can. Why not see?

—— 93 ——

A Question of Balance

"The generous person doesn't expect anything in return.
The over-giver doesn't expect anything in return either—
except to be petted and feted and praised and loved
unconditionally for the rest of time."
—Elizabeth Gilbert

My wife is terrific. In the few years we've been together, she's helped me give up cigarettes and hard liquor; taught me how to appreciate music, literature, and the arts; taught me how to cook gourmet meals and enjoy fine wine; and helped me improve my appearance, all of which have given me tremendous self-confidence. So now I want a divorce. Frankly, I'm too good for her.

LIFE LESSON

It's easy to vilify this guy, because he's bragging about being a self-centered jerk—in fact, that's what's funny. But instead, think about the wife, who seems to just give, give, give without checking in to see how her gifts are being received. She doesn't seem to realize that if the other person in a relationship doesn't appreciate your efforts, then you're not building a stronger connection—you're creating an imbalance that can undermine the whole thing.

A relationship is a two-way street. Make sure things are flowing to you as well as from you. If there's no give and take, you could be giving it all away . . . and wind up with nothing.

BEYOND THE PUNCH LINE

Are *you* giving too much? Here are some questions you can ask yourself to help figure it out:

1. **Do you expect something in return?** Is giving just a tool to be appreciated, loved, liked, or admired? If you don't get what you want in return, does giving leave you feeling empty and alone?

2. **Are you denying a part of yourself by giving?** Rather than taking care of yourself, are you sacrificing your emotional needs in favor of someone else's? The flip side: Do you have a hard time accepting something in return without feeling guilty?

3. **Are you afraid to stop giving?** Do you think people will be unhappy or admit they're not really interested if you stop?

4. **Do you feel compelled to give constantly?** Do you find yourself apologizing when you can't give as much as you'd like?

5. **Do you know, deep down, that something's wrong?** Most of us know much more about ourselves than we admit. If you're suspicious about your own motives, chances are you already know that you're giving for the wrong reasons.

—— 94 ——

Badge of Shame

"I wish I could buy you for what you are really worth
and sell you for what you think you're worth.
I sure would make money on the deal."
—Zora Neale Hurston

A local DEA agent stops at a farm and tells the old farmer, "I have to inspect your fields for marijuana."

"Okay," says the farmer, "but don't go in that field over there," and points out the location.

The agent explodes, waving his badge and shouting, "Listen, friend. This badge means I can go anywhere I choose, on any land, no questions asked. Get it?"

The farmer nods politely, apologizes, and returns to his chores. A short time later, he hears loud screams and sees the agent running for his life, chased by a huge bull. The farmer throws down his tools, runs to the fence, and yells at the top of his lungs, "Your badge! Show him your badge!"

LIFE LESSON

Arrogance and self-importance will get you nowhere—except maybe into trouble. Everything works better when you show consideration, friendliness, and respect to the folks you deal with, because in the end, no matter how much authority you think you have, you still need people's cooperation and good will to succeed.

BEYOND THE PUNCH LINE

Do people perceive you as arrogant? Here are six habits associated with arrogance. Do they describe you?

1. You're a name-dropper.
Possible perception: You're trying to show that you're more important than "ordinary" people.

2. You constantly interrupt people in conversation.
Possible perception: You don't care what others have to say; you consider your views more important than theirs.

3. You consistently arrive late.
Possible perception: Your time is more valuable than anyone else's. That goes double if you never apologize for your lateness.

4. You take credit for good outcomes and blame others for bad ones.
Possible perception: You need to establish your "superiority" at other people's expense. You can't accept that others are worthy of the same recognition.

5. You use "dominant" body language—swagger when you walk, move into people's body space, point aggressively, etc.
Possible perception: You get off on intimidating people.

6. You always insist you're right.

Possible perception: You think you're smarter than other people. You have no interest in learning; every conversation is just a competition and *you* have to win.

— 95 —

Nun the Wiser

"I was so embarrassed, I could feel my nerves curling like bacon over a hot fire."
—Margaret Halsey

The mother superior of a convent was working at her desk one swelteringly hot August day. The air-conditioning in the office was broken, and she was very uncomfortable in her full habit, so she decided to take off her clothes and work in the nude. It was a dangerous thing to do but, after all, who would know? A few minutes later there was a knock at her door and one of the other nuns announced: "Mother Superior, there's a blind man to see you."

The nun panicked . . . but then realized that a blind man wouldn't be able to see that she was naked. So she opened the door and said, "Come in. Nice to see you."

The man looked at her and replied, "Nice to see you too. Where do you want me to hang these blinds?"

LIFE LESSON

Most embarrassing situations aren't quite this extreme. But when you're the one who's embarrassed, you probably feel just as naked as the mother superior. Unfortunately, there's no way to undo a faux pas, but if you deal with it in the moment, you can probably minimize its impact. That's also true if you're in the position of the "blind man." By acting quickly (and generously), you can make it easy for the embarrassed person to get past the experience. They'll appreciate it, and you'll feel good that you could help. No matter how you do it, successfully navigating an embarrassing situation is good for everyone's self-esteem.

BEYOND THE PUNCH LINE

Have you ever tripped and fallen, ripped your pants, forgotten someone's name, had your car stall out in the middle of an intersection, farted in a crowd, or spilled a drink? Researchers say these are among the most embarrassing situations for most people. Here are a few tips to get you through one—or any—of them:

• **Stay calm.** One of the reasons embarrassing situations can be tense is that they evoke *other* people's anxieties. If you can reduce an observer's anxiety, there's a good chance you'll reduce the immediate impact of your faux pas.

• **Use humor.** A 2012 scientific study showed that the most effective way to smooth out an embarrassing situation is with humor. Laughing at yourself simultaneously acknowledges the event, relieves the tension, and lets people know you're not taking it too seriously (which means *they* don't have to). "You don't have to be a professional comedian to know how to use humor in an awkward situation," says one psychologist. "Even saying 'Awkward!' can do the trick."

• **Apologize.** If you did something *to* someone, a sincere apology can set things right. But excessive apologizing is counterproductive. It doesn't allow you (or them) to move past the embarrassment—and it doesn't sound genuine.

• **Change the subject.** If you do something embarrassing that no one really notices—or that doesn't bother anyone except you—try changing the subject instead of calling attention to it. Most of us have short attention spans, and we'll follow along willingly. Remember: Completely ignoring an embarrassing situation usually doesn't work. This only applies to minor embarrassments.

96

Mob Rule

"I'm in with the 'in' crowd.
And I know what the 'in' crowd knows."
—"The 'In' Crowd," lyrics by Billy Page

A man from the big city is traveling out west and one night he goes into a cowboy bar. He's having a few beers when someone walks into the crowded saloon and shouts, "Every damn Republican is a horse's ass!" The patrons immediately swarm the guy, beat him up, and throw him into the street.

The city man can't believe what he just saw, but before he can say anything to the bartender, another guy comes into the bar and shouts, "Every damn Democrat is a horse's ass!" Once again, the patrons swarm the guy, beat him up, and toss him into the street.

The city man is stunned. He finally turns to the bartender and says, "I don't get it. Are you guys Democrats or Republicans?"

"Neither," says the bartender, "we're horse people."

LIFE LESSON
You may not know what group someone belongs to, but you can be pretty sure they identify with some group. Studies show

that we derive a big share of our sense of social identity from a connection to the groups we relate to—and the ones we don't.

Practically speaking, this means you can learn a lot about what people believe—and how they'll behave—just by knowing what groups they belong to. And conversely, if you know what an individual considers their self-interest you can make an educated guess about which groups they feel are their cohorts.

This approach isn't foolproof, no one is entirely predictable, but the values that connect a person to "their" group provide a pretty accurate window into their inner life. You ignore them at your own peril.

BEYOND THE PUNCH LINE

In the late 1970s, two British psychologists, Henri Tajfel and John Turner, came up with *social identity theory* to explain human group behavior. Their hypothesis: Belonging to a group is a critical part of human existence—not something false or superficial. The psychologists described the "joining experience" as a three-stage process.

1. **Social categorization.** First, we put people in definable categories: black, white, Latino, Christian, Muslim, disabled, blue-collar, white-collar, and so forth. There's no special meaning to this—it's just part of a human tendency to categorize everything around us in order to make it comprehensible. But it's also the beginning of seeing people as group members rather than just individuals. At this point, however, there's no implied conflict between groups.

2. **Social identification.** We start to identify overtly with a particular group (or groups). This is the "in-group"; the groups to which we don't belong are now the "out-groups." We begin to adopt the norms and attitudes of the in-group, dressing, acting, and speaking like our fellow group members.

3. **Social comparison.** Now things start to get charged. Our self-esteem becomes tied up with the status of our group. And since there's really no way to measure this status except in comparison to other groups, we become invested in establishing the in-group's superiority—and the out-group's inferiority. We tend to minimize the differences between in-group members, and exaggerate differences with the out-group.

This *can* be the beginning of prejudice and discrimination, but it isn't inevitable. If we feel society is fair and legitimate, we're more likely to devote ourselves to improving our group's status by developing its positive characteristics than by tearing other groups down. It's only when we feel the system is unfair that we're more likely to become competitive with other groups, challenge the status quo, and try to effect social and political change.

97

The Memory Hole

"You don't remember what happened.
What you remember becomes *what happened."*
—John Green

An elderly husband and wife are having difficulty remembering things, so they go to a doctor to make sure nothing's wrong. The doctor examines them and says, "Physically, you're in great health, but if you need help with your memory, a lot of people your age find it useful to write little notes to themselves as reminders."

That night while they're watching TV, the husband gets up and the wife asks where he's going.

"I'm going to the kitchen for a glass of water," he says.

"While you're there, will you get me some ice cream?" she says.

"Sure. Vanilla?" he says.

"Yes, but maybe you should write it down," she says.

"I don't have to write it down. You want vanilla ice cream, right?"

"Yes," she says, "and I'd like strawberries and whipped cream on it. Do you want to write it down?"

"I don't have to write it down. You want vanilla ice cream with strawberries and whipped cream," he says, and walks into the kitchen.

Twenty minutes later he returns to the living room and hands his wife a plate of bacon and eggs.

"Hey!" she says. "Where's my toast?"

LIFE LESSON

You may think memory is just a problem for old folks. There's no question that our memory does get worse as we get older, but researchers are discovering that it's not so great to begin with. Science has proven that we all invent at least some of what we "remember"—and then we can't tell the difference between what we've fabricated and what really happened. So no matter how old you are, you can't trust your memory completely—even if you're *sure* it's reliable.

The next time you get into a disagreement with someone about who remembers an event more accurately, don't take it too seriously. There's a good chance that neither of you remembers it exactly right. Just pick the "memory" that works the best for both of you, and move on.

BEYOND THE PUNCH LINE

Scientists say that one third of your memory loss is genetic— which means you can still influence the other 65 percent of memory with some pretty easy tricks. Here are four simple ways to remember something more accurately:

1. **Focus on it for at least eight seconds.** That's the minimum it takes for your brain to "encode" (learn) information. Create an environment in which you can concentrate intensely for at least that long. Avoid distractions. According to several experts, "How you pay attention to information may be the most important factor in how much of it you actually remember."

2. **Connect it to existing memories.** Studies show we're more likely to retain new information if we can relate it to something we already know. For example: You're more likely to remember the contents of a photo if it was taken in a place you've been; and you're more likely to remember an address if you relate it to a street you know.

3. **Use the "chunking" technique.** Most of us can only retain four to seven items in our short-term memory. But we can increase the amount of information contained in those items by grouping several bits of info into one item. For example: A seven-digit phone number can be remembered as one word by using the corresponding letters on the dial pad.

4. **Use everything you've got.** Get as many of your senses into the process as possible. You'll remember more if you connect the information to smells, tastes, textures, and colors.

98

Dream Job

*"I find my life is a lot easier the lower
I keep everyone's expectations."*
—Bill Watterson

A recent college graduate is applying for a job at a big company and the interviewer asks him what kind of salary he's looking for.

"I was thinking around $125,000 a year," replies the applicant. "Maybe higher, depending on how generous your benefits are."

"Well," the interviewer says, "how about this: We'll start you at $130,000, enroll you in our executive medical plan with full vision and dental, give you a corner office, eight weeks' paid vacation a year, and your own company car—a brand-new Mercedes."

"Wow!" says the applicant. "Are you kidding?"

"Yeah," replies the interviewer, "but you started it."

LIFE LESSON

Unless you ask for what you want, you're certainly not going to get it—so it's good to aim high. But there's a thin line between an ambitious goal and embarrassing overreach. When your goals are obviously unrealistic, they can boomerang on you. People (like the interviewer in the joke) will see right through them, and won't take you seriously. And on a larger scale, unrealistic expectations can distort your view of what's really possible in life, preventing you from finding satisfaction in your job or relationships. So be ambitious, but be careful. Your expectations define your interactions with the world, and if they're unreasonable, they'll only make your life more difficult.

BEYOND THE PUNCH LINE

The hardest part of letting go of unrealistic expectations is figuring out which ones are unrealistic—especially if you've been holding on to them for a long time. Here are some ideas that might help:

• **Pretend you're advising someone else.** You can probably evaluate your expectations more objectively if you imagine they're being held by a relative or close friend instead of you. Be as honest with yourself as you'd be with them.

• **Are your expectations too rigid?** Realistic expectations will change as circumstances change. If you're unable to adjust your expectations when something new and unexpected happens, it's a good indication they're unrealistic.

• **Examine the results.** Unrealistic expectations can never be met—that's what "unrealistic" means. Result: They'll always leave you feeling disappointed. So if an expectation consistently disappoints you, consider it unrealistic.

99

First Things First

"The older I get, the more wisdom I find in the ancient
rule of taking first things first, a process which
often reduces the most complex human problem
to a manageable proportion."
—Dwight D. Eisenhower

A man buys a parakeet, but is very disappointed to find that it won't talk. So he goes back to the pet shop. "Maybe he needs stimulation," the store owner says, and suggests putting a mirror in the cage so the parakeet can see itself. The man tries that, but the bird still won't talk ... so he goes back to the pet shop again. The owner suggests putting a ladder and a bell in the cage so that the parakeet can climb up and ring the bell. The man tries that, but the bird still won't talk ... so he goes back to the pet shop again. The owner suggests putting a cuttlefish bone in the cage so that the parakeet can have something to peck at. The man tries that, but the bird still won't talk ... so he goes back to the pet shop again. "I don't know what to say," the owner apologizes. "Maybe it was just a nontalking bird." Disappointed, the man goes back home ... but as he walks through the door, he hears the parakeet speaking. He rushes to the cage just in time to hear the parakeet say, with its dying breath, "Doesn't that f***ing pet shop sell any birdseed?"

LIFE LESSON

Would someone really forget something as obvious as feeding their pet? Well, think about your own life. How often have you lost sight of simple priorities and inadvertently "killed" something you cared about? There's no limit to the array of things you can screw up when you get your priorities wrong—from forgetting to pay a bill to torpedoing a romantic relationship.

So first things first: Learn to prioritize. Success—and sometimes even survival—depends on it. It's an essential life skill that will apply to practically everything you ever try to do—and it will ultimately reduce the number of "parakeets" you have to bury.

BEYOND THE PUNCH LINE

There are many approaches to prioritizing, but all of them involve two basic steps:

1. **Create a master list.** Start with a list of all the things you want or need to accomplish. Don't rank them yet; that comes later. Some experts recommend listing *anything* that takes time, including all routine tasks and calendar items. They also suggest that you do your list in advance—for example, if it's a daily list, then write tomorrow's list today. The reason: It's much harder to make a good list when you're distracted by new demands.

2. **Organize your tasks.** Usually this entails sorting them by urgency and importance (urgent = needs immediate attention). For example:

• MITs. One system suggests picking the three "MITs" (Most Important Things) from the list to do first. When those are complete, you can attack other tasks at will, as a sort of bonus. The next day, if it's a daily list (or next week, if it's a weekly list), pick three new MITs. Some experts recommend making one of them something that advances a long-term goal.

• The Pareto principle. Also called the 80-20 rule—the general observation that "the majority of results come from a minority of inputs." Applied to prioritizing, it translates as "20 percent of your work accounts for 80 percent of your result." So the task is to identify the most productive 20 percent and make those items your number-one priorities. One way to narrow it down is to keep asking yourself, "If I could only do one task on my list, which would it be?"

• The Eisenhower method. Named for President Dwight Eisenhower, who made his to-do lists by drawing four boxes and labeling them Urgent and Important, Important but not Urgent, Urgent but not Important, and Not Urgent or Important. Then he put each task from the master list in the appropriate box, and he could see what his real priorities were. Writer James Clear simplifies the process by calling the boxes "Do (Do it now), Decide (Schedule a time to do it), Delegate (Who can do it for you?), and Delete (Eliminate)."

And in the End

"If at first you don't succeed, try, try again. Then quit.
There's no point in being a damn fool about it."
—W. C. Fields

A guy takes his date to a dinner at the local country club. It's an unusual setup: People have to wait in separate lines for each type of food. As his date sits down, the guy volunteers to go get their dinner. First he waits in the line for the roast beef. Then he waits in the line for potatoes. Then he waits in the vegetable line, the bread line, and the gravy line. Finally he brings back two full plates of food. "What would you like to drink?" he asks.

"A glass of punch would be nice," she says. So he goes to get it. He scouts around and finds a line for wine, a line for beer, a line for soda, and even a line for milk. But after a while he gives up.

LIFE LESSON
Sometimes there's just no punch line.

"Humor is just another defense against the universe."
—Mel Brooks

Special thanks to Max Hittesdorf, Irving Lubliner,
Jay Newman, Sophie the Muse, Gene Burnett, John Dollison,
Maggie, Sharon, Lorrie B, Pony Espresso (aka "the office"),
Suzie Bolotin, and our editor, Bruce "Mr. Patience" Tracy.